SAT 4000

NOVA PRESS

JEFF KOLBY

Additional educational titles from Nova Press (available at novapress.net):

- ➤ **SAT Prep Course** (640 pages, includes software)
  SAT Math Prep Course (404 pages)
- ➤ **ACT Math Prep Course** (402 pages)
- ➤ **GRE Prep Course** (624 pages, includes software)
  GRE Math Prep Course (528 pages)
- ➤ **GMAT Prep Course** (624 pages, includes software)
  GMAT Math Prep Course (528 pages)
  GMAT Data Sufficiency Prep Course (422 pages)
- ➤ **Master The LSAT** (608 pages, includes software & 4 official LSAT exams)
- ➤ **The MCAT Physics Book** (444 pages)
  The MCAT Biology Book (416 pages)
  The MCAT Chemistry Book (428 pages)
- ➤ **Speaking and Writing Strategies for the TOEFL® iBT:** (394 pages, includes audio CD)
  500 Words, Phrases, and Idioms for the TOEFL® iBT: (238 pages, includes audio CD)
- ➤ **Law School Basics:** A Preview of Law School and Legal Reasoning (224 pages)

ISBN-10: 1–889057–79–7
ISBN-13: 978–1–889057–79–8

Nova Press
11659 Mayfield Ave., Suite 1
Los Angeles, CA 90049

Phone: 1-800-949-6175
E-mail: info@novapress.net
Website: www.novapress.net

Contents

Contents

About This Book

The SAT tests a surprisingly limited number of words. In the following list, you will find words that occur frequently on the SAT. Granted, memorizing a list of words is rather dry, but it is probably the most effective way to improve your performance on the reading section.

Over the years, this list of 4000 words has been an invaluable tool for students who have both the time and the determination to wade through it. It's chock-full of words that are prime candidates for the SAT.

Whenever possible, one-word definitions are used. Although this makes a definition less precise, it also makes it easier to remember. Many common words appear in the list of words, but with their less common meanings. For example, the common meaning of *champion* is "winner." A less common meaning for *champion* is to support or fight for someone else. (Think of the phrase "to champion a cause.") This is the meaning that would be used in the list.

As you read through the list of words, mark any that you do not know with a check mark. Then when you read through the list again, mark any that you do not remember with two checks. Continue in this manner until you have learned the words.

There are four types of quizzes interspersed in the word list: Matching, Antonyms, Analogies, and Sentence Completions. The Matching quizzes, review words that were just introduced. All the other quizzes contain words from any part of the list.

THE
WORDS

A

a cappella without accompaniment

à la carte priced separately

a priori reasoning based on general principles

aback unexpected, surprised

abacus counting device

abandon desert, forsake

abase degrade

abash humiliate, embarrass

abate lessen, subside

abatement alleviation

abbey monastery

abbreviate shorten

abdicate relinquish power or position

abdomen belly

abduct kidnap

aberrant abnormal

abet aid, encourage (typically of crime)

abeyance postponement

abhor detest

abide submit, endure

abject wretched

abjure renounce

ablate cut away

ablution cleansing

abode home

abolish annul, eliminate

abominable detestable

aboriginal indigenous, native

abortive unsuccessful

abound be plentiful

abreast side-by-side

abridge shorten

abroad overseas

abrogate cancel

abrupt ending suddenly

abscess infected and inflamed tissue

abscond to run away (secretly)

absolve acquit, free from blame

abstain refrain

abstract theoretical, intangible

abstruse difficult to understand

abut touch, border on

abysmal deficient, sub par

abyss chasm

academy school

accede yield, agree

accentuate emphasize

accession attainment of rank

accessory attachment, accomplice

acclaim recognition, fame

acclimate accustom oneself to a climate, adjust

acclivity ascent, incline

accolade applause, tribute

accommodate adapt, assist, house

accomplice one who aids a lawbreaker

accord agreement

accost to approach and speak to someone aggressively

accouter equip, clothe

accredit authorize

accrete grow larger

accrue accumulate

accumulate amass

acerbic caustic, bitter (of speech)

acme summit, zenith

acolyte assistant (usually to clergy)

acoustic pertaining to sound

acquaint familiarize

acquiesce agree passively

acquit free from blame

acrid pungent, caustic, choking

acrimonious caustic, bitter, resentful

acrophobia fear of heights

actuate induce, start

acumen insight

acute sharp, intense

ad nauseam to a ridiculous degree

ad-lib improvise

adage proverb

adamant insistent

adapt adjust to changing conditions

adaptable pliable

addendum appendix, supplement

adduce offer as example

adept skillful

adhere stick to

adherent supporter

adieu farewell

adipose fatty

adjacent next to

adjourn suspend, discontinue

adjudicate judge

adjunct addition

administer manage

admissible allowable

admonish warn gently

ado fuss, commotion

Adonis a beautiful man

adroit skillful

adulation applause, worship

adulterate contaminate, corrupt

adumbration overshadow

advent arrival of something important

adventitious accidental, extrinsic

adversary opponent

adverse unfavorable, opposing

adversity hardship

advise give counsel

advocate urge, support

aegis that which protects, sponsorship

aerial pertaining to the air

aerobics exercise

Quiz 1 (Matching)

Match each word in the first column with its definition in the second column.
Answers are on page 101.

1.	ABASE	A.	applause
2.	ABSTAIN	B.	caustic
3.	ACOLYTE	C.	shorten
4.	ABEYANCE	D.	applause
5.	ABRIDGE	E.	assistant
6.	ACCOLADE	F.	postponement
7.	ACRIMONIOUS	G.	refrain
8.	ADDUCE	H.	exercise
9.	ADULATION	I.	degrade
10.	AEROBICS	J.	offer as example

aesthetic pleasing to the senses, beautiful

affable friendly

affect influence

affectation pretense, showing off

affidavit sworn written statement

affiliate associate

affiliation connection, association

affinity fondness

affix fasten

affliction illness

affluent abundant, wealthy

affray brawl

affront insult

aficionado devotee, ardent follower

afoul entangled, in trouble

aft rear

aftermath consequence

agape wonder

agenda plan, timetable

agent provocateur agitator

aggrandize exaggerate

aggravate worsen

aggregate total, collect

aggressor attacker

aggrieve mistreat

aggrieved unjustly injured

aghast horrified

agile nimble

agitate stir up

agnate related on the father's side

agnostic not knowing whether God exists

agrarian pertaining to farming

agronomy science of crop production

air discuss, broadcast

airs pretension

akimbo with hands on hips

akin related

al fresco outdoors

alacrity swiftness

albatross large sea bird

albino lacking pigmentation

alcove recess, niche

alias assumed name

alibi excuse

alienate estrange, antagonize

alight land, descend, to happen to find a place to rest

allay to reassure

allege assert without proof

allegiance loyalty

allegory fable

allegro fast

alleviate lessen, assuage

alliteration repetition of the same sound

allocate distribute

allot allocate, ration

allude refer to indirectly

ally unite for a purpose

almanac calendar with additional information

alms charity

aloof arrogant, detached

altercation argument

altitude height

alto low female voice

altruism benevolence, generosity

amalgamation mixture

amass collect

ambient surrounding, environment

ambiguous unclear

ambivalence conflicting emotions

ambulatory able to walk

ameliorate improve

amenable agreeable

amend correct

amenities courtesies, comforts

amenity pleasantness

amiable friendly

amid among

amiss wrong, out of place

amity friendship, good will

amnesty pardon

amoral without morals

amorous loving, sexual

amorphous shapeless

amortize pay by installments

amphibious able to operate in water and land

amphitheater oval-shaped theater

amuck murderous frenzy

amulet charm, talisman

amuse entertain

anachronistic out of historical order

anaerobic without oxygen

anagram a word formed by rearranging the letters of another word

analgesic pain-soother

Quiz 2 (Antonyms)

Directions: Choose the word most opposite in meaning to the capitalized word. Answers are on page 101.

1. GRATUITOUS: (A) voluntary   (B) arduous   (C) solicitous   (D) righteous   (E) befitting

2. FALLOW: (A) fatuous   (B) productive   (C) bountiful   (D) pertinacious   (E) opprobrious

3. METTLE: (A) ad hoc   (B) perdition   (C) woe   (D) trepidation   (E) apathy

4. SAVANT: (A) dolt   (B) sage   (C) attaché   (D) apropos comment   (E) state of confusion

5. RIFE: (A) multitudinous   (B) blemished   (C) sturdy   (D) counterfeit   (E) sparse

6. ABRIDGE: (A) distend   (B) assail   (C) unfetter   (D) enfeeble   (E) prove

7. PRODIGAL: (A) bountiful   (B) dependent   (C) provident   (D) superfluous   (E) profligate

8. REQUIEM: (A) humility   (B) prerequisite   (C) resolution   (D) reign   (E) hiatus

9. METE: (A) indict   (B) convoke   (C) hamper   (D) disseminate   (E) deviate

10. SEVERANCE: (A) continuation   (B) dichotomy   (C) astringency   (D) disclosure   (E) remonstrance

---

analogous similar

analogy point by point comparison

anarchist terrorist, nihilist

anarchy absence of government, chaos

anathema curse, abomination

anecdote story

aneurysm bulging in a blood vessel

angst anxiety, dread

animadversion critical remark

animated exuberant

animosity dislike

animus hate

annals historical records

annex to attach, to take possession of

annihilate destroy

annotate to add explanatory notes

annul cancel

annular ring-shaped

anodyne pain soothing

anoint consecrate, apply ointment

anomalous abnormal

anonymity state of being anonymous

antagonistic hostile

antagonize harass

antechamber waiting room

antediluvian ancient, obsolete

anthology collection

anthrax disease, bacterium

antic caper, prank

antipathy repulsion, hated

antipodal exactly opposite

antiquated outdated, obsolete

antiquity ancient times

antithesis direct opposite

apartheid racial segregation

apathetic unconcerned, uninterested

apathy indifference

ape mimic

aperture opening

apex highest point

aphasia speechless

aphorism maxim

aplomb poise

apocalyptic ominous, doomed

apocryphal of doubtful authenticity

apoplexy stroke

apostate one who abandons one's faith

apotheosis deification

appall horrify

apparition phantom

appease pacify

appellation title

append affix

apposite apt

apprehensive anxious, worried

apprise inform

approbation approval

apropos appropriate

apt suitable

aptitude ability

aquatic pertaining to water

arbiter judge

arbitrament final judgment

arbitrary tyrannical, capricious

arcane secret, difficult to understand

archaic antiquated

archetype original model, epitome

archipelago group of island

archives public records

ardent passionate

ardor passion

arduous hard

Argonauts gold-seekers, adventurers

argot specialized vocabulary, jargon

aria operatic song

arid dry, dull

aristocrat nobleman

armada fleet of ships

armistice truce

arraign indict

array arrangement

arrears in debt

arrogate seize without right

arroyo gully

arsenal supply, stockpile of weapons

artful skillful, cunning

articulate well-spoken

artifice trick

artless naive, simple

ascend rise

ascendancy powerful state

ascertain discover

ascetic self-denying

ascribe to attribute

aseptic sterile

ashen pale

asinine stupid

askance to view with suspicion

askew crooked

aspersion slander

asphyxiate suffocate

aspirant contestant

aspiration ambition

assail attack

assassin murderer

assent agree

assert affirm

assess appraise

assiduous hard-working

assimilate absorb, integrate

assonance partial rhyme

assuage lessen (pain)

astral pertaining to stars

astringent causing contraction, severe

astute wise

asunder apart, into separate parts

asylum place of refuge

asymmetric uneven

atavistic exhibiting the characteristics of one's forebears

atelier workshop

atoll reef

atomize vaporize

atone make amends

atrophy the wasting away of muscle

attenuate weaken, assuage

attest testify

attire dress

attribute ascribe

attrition deterioration, reduction

Quiz 3 (Matching)

Match each word in the first column with its definition in the second column.
Answers are on page 101.

1.	ANATHEMA	A.	hard
2.	ANNIHILATE	B.	curse
3.	ANOMALOUS	C.	gully
4.	APATHETIC	D.	suffocate
5.	ARCHAIC	E.	antiquated
6.	ARDUOUS	F.	destroy
7.	ARROYO	G.	abnormal
8.	ASPHYXIATE	H.	unconcerned
9.	ASTRINGENT	I.	make amends
10.	ATONE	J.	causing contraction

atypical abnormal

au courant well informed, chic

audacity boldness

audient listening, attentive

audition tryout

augment increase, supplement

augur predict

august noble, majestic

aura atmosphere, emanation

auspices patronage, protection

auspicious favorable

austere harsh, Spartan

authorize grant, sanction

automaton robot

autonomous self-governing

auxiliary secondary, supportive

avail assistance

avant garde vanguard

avarice greed

avatar incarnation

averse loath, reluctant

avert turn away

avian pertaining to birds

avid enthusiastic

avocation hobby

avouch attest, guarantee

avow declare

avuncular like an uncle

awry crooked

axiom self-evident truth

aye affirmative vote

azure sky blue

B

babbittry smugness

bacchanal orgy, drunken celebration

badger pester

badinage banter

bagatelle nonentity, trifle

bailiwick area of concern or business

baleen whalebone

baleful hostile, malignant

balk hesitate

balky hesitant

ballad song

ballast counterbalance

ballistics study of projectiles

balm soothing ointment

banal trite

bandy exchange

bane poison, nuisance

barbarian savage

bard poet

baroque ornate

barrister lawyer

bask take pleasure in, sun

basso low male voice

bastion fort

bathos sentimentality

batten fasten, board up

battery physical attack

bauble trinket

beatify sanctify

beatitude state of bliss

beckon lure

becoming proper

bedlam uproar

befit to be suitable

beget produce, procreate

begrudge resent, envy

beguile deceive, seduce

behemoth monster

behest command

beholden in debt, obliged

belabor assail verbally, dwell on

belated delayed, overdue

beleaguer besiege

belfry bell tower

belie misrepresent, disprove

belittle disparage

bellicose warlike

belligerent combative

bellow shout

bellwether leader, guide

bemoan lament

bemused bewildered

benchmark standard

benediction blessing

benefactor patron

benevolent kind

benign harmless

bent determined

bequeath will

bequest gift, endowment

berate scold

bereave to rob, to deprive somebody of a love one, especially through death

Quiz 4 (Antonyms)

<u>Directions:</u> Choose the word most opposite in meaning to the capitalized word. Answers are on page 101.

1. HYPOCRITICAL: (A) forthright   (B) judicious   (C) circumspect
    (D) puritanical   (E) unorthodox

2. VOLUMINOUS: (A) obscure   (B) cantankerous   (C) unsubstantial
    (D) tenacious   (E) opprobrious

3. FANATICISM: (A) delusion   (B) fascism   (C) remorse
    (D) cynicism   (E) indifference

4. INTERMINABLE: (A) finite   (B) jejune   (C) tranquil
    (D) incessant   (E) imprudent

5. ORNATE: (A) Spartan   (B) blemished   (C) sturdy
    (D) counterfeit   (E) temporary

6. MUTABILITY: (A) simplicity   (B) apprehension   (C) frailty
    (D) maverick   (E) tenacity

7. VIRULENT: (A) benign   (B) intrepid   (C) malignant
    (D) hyperbolic   (E) tentative

8. ABSTEMIOUS: (A) timely   (B) immoderate   (C) bellicose
    (D) servile   (E) irreligious

9. VERBOSE: (A) subliminal   (B) myopic   (C) pithy
    (D) dauntless   (E) ubiquitous

10. VISCID: (A) subtle   (B) faint   (C) slick   (D) vicious
    (E) difficult

---

bereft deprived of

berserk crazed with anger

beseech implore, beg

beset harass, encircle

besiege beleaguer, surround

besmirch slander, sully

bespeak attest

bestial beast-like, brutal

bestow offer, grant

betrothed engaged

bevy group

bibliography list of sources of information

bicameral having two legislative branches

bicker quarrel

biennial occurring every two years

bilateral two-sided

bilious ill-tempered

bilk swindle

biodegradable naturally decaying

biopsy removing tissue for examination

biped two-footed animal

bistro tavern, cafe

bivouac encampment

blandish flatter, grovel

blasé bored with life

blasphemy insulting God

bleak cheerless, forlorn

blight decay

bliss happiness

blithe joyous

bloated swollen

bode portend

bogus forged, false

bogy bugbear

boisterous noisy

bolt move quickly and suddenly

bombast pompous speech

bon vivant gourmet, epicure

bona fide made in good faith

bonanza a stroke of luck

boon payoff, windfall

boor vulgar person

bootless unavailing

booty loot, stolen goods

botch bungle

bourgeois middle class

bovine cow-like

boycott abstain in protest

bracing refreshing

brackish salty

brandish display menacingly

bravado feigned bravery

bravura technically difficult, brilliant

brawn strength

brevity shortness of expression

brigand robber

brink edge, threshold

broach bring up a topic for conversation

bromide cliché

brook tolerate

browbeat to bully

brusque curt

bucolic rustic

buffet blow, pummel

buffoon fool, joker

bulwark fortification

buncombe empty, showy talk

buoyant floatable, cheerful

burgeon sprout

burlesque farce

burly husky

buttress support

C

cabal a group of conspirators

cabaret night club

cache hiding place

cachet prestige

cacophony dissonance, harsh noise

cadaver corpse

cadaverous haggard

cadence rhythm

cadet a student of a military academy

cadge beg

cadre small group

cajole encourage, coax

calamity disaster

calculating scheming

caliber ability, character

callous insensitive

callow inexperienced

calumny slander

camaraderie fellowship

canaille rabble

canard hoax

candid frank, unrehearsed

candor frankness

canine pertaining to dogs

canon rule

cant insincere speech

cantankerous peevish

cantata musical composition

canvass survey

capacious spacious

capillary thin tube

capital most significant, pertaining to wealth

capitol legislative building

capitulate surrender

capricious fickle, impulsive

caption title

captious fond of finding fault in others

captivate engross, fascinate

carafe bottle

carbine rifle

carcinogenic causing cancer

carcinoma tumor

cardinal chief

cardiologist one who studies the heart

careen swerve

carrion decaying flesh

cartographer mapmaker

cascade waterfall

cashmere fine wool from Asia

Cassandra unheeded prophet

castigate criticize

castrate remove the testicles

Quiz 5 (Matching)

Match each word in the first column with its definition in the second column.
Answers are on page 101.

1.	BESMIRCH	A.	unheeded prophet
2.	BICAMERAL	B.	peevish
3.	BILATERAL	C.	pertaining to dogs
4.	BOOTLESS	D.	plot
5.	BRANDISH	E.	farce
6.	BURLESQUE	F.	display menacingly
7.	CABAL	G.	unavailing
8.	CANINE	H.	two-sided
9.	CANTANKEROUS	I.	having two legislative branches
10.	CASSANDRA	J.	sully

casuistry specious reasoning

cataclysm catastrophe

catastrophic disastrous

categorical absolute, certain

cathartic purgative, purifying

catholic universal, worldly

caucus meeting

cause célèbre celebrated legal case

caustic scathing (of speech)

cauterize to sear

cavalier disdainful, nonchalant

caveat warning

caveat emptor buyer beware

cavil quibble

cavort frolic

cede transfer ownership, relinquish

celestial heavenly

celibate abstaining from sex

cenotaph empty tomb, monument

censorious condemning speech

censure condemn

ceramics pottery

cerebral pertaining to the brain

cessation a stopping

chafe abrade

chagrin embarrassment

chalice goblet

champion defend

chaperon escort

charade pantomime, sham

charlatan quack, imposter

chartreuse greenish yellow

chary cautious

chaste pure, virgin

chasten castigate

chateau castle

cheeky brass, forward

cherub cupid

cherubic sweet, innocent

chicanery trickery

chide scold

chimerical imaginary, dreamlike

choleric easily angered

chortle laugh, snort

chronic continual (usually of illness)

chronicle a history, record

chronology arrangement by time

churl a boor

chutzpah gall

Cimmerian dim, unlit

cipher zero, nobody, a code

circa about (of time)

circuitous roundabout

circumcise remove the foreskin

circumlocution roundabout expression

circumspect cautious

circumvent evade, thwart

citadel fortress

citation summons to appear in court

clamor noise

clan extended family

clandestine secret

claustrophobia fear of enclosed places

cleave split

cleft split

clemency forgiveness

clique a small group

cloister refuge, monastery

clone duplicate

clout influence

cloven split

cloy glut, to sicken by excess

cloyed jaded

co-opt preempt, usurp

coagulate thicken

coalesce combine

coda concluding passage

coddle pamper

codicil supplement to a will

coercion force

coffer strong box

cogent well-put, convincing

cogitate ponder

cognate from the same source

cognizant aware, mindful

cognomen family name

cohabit live together

cohere stick together

cohort an associate

coiffure hairdo

collaborate work together

collar seize, arrest

collateral securities for a debt

colloquial informal speech

colloquy conference

collusion conspiracy

colonnade row of columns

Quiz 6 (Antonyms)

Directions: Choose the word most opposite in meaning to the capitalized word. Answers are on page 101.

1. DERISION: (A) urgency   (B) admonishment   (C) uniqueness
                 (D) diversity   (E) acclaim

2. ANTIPATHY: (A) fondness   (B) disagreement   (C) boorishness
                 (D) provocation   (E) opprobrium

3. CAJOLE: (A) implore   (B) glance at   (C) belittle
                 (D) ennoble   (E) engender

4. CENSURE: (A) prevaricate   (B) titillate   (C) aggrandize
                 (D) obscure   (E) sanction

5. ADULATION: (A) immutability   (B) reluctance   (C) reflection
                 (D) defamation   (E) indifference

6. NOISOME: (A) salubrious   (B) affable   (C) multifarious
                 (D) provident   (E) officious

7. CONSECRATE: (A) curb   (B) destroy   (C) curse
                 (D) inveigh   (E) exculpate

8. ILLUSTRIOUS: (A) bellicose   (B) ignoble   (C) theoretical
                 (D) esoteric   (E) immaculate

9. DEIGN: (A) inveigh   (B) gainsay   (C) speculate   (D) reject
            (E) laud

10. SUBTERFUGE: (A) bewilderment   (B) artlessness   (C) deceit
                  (D) felicitation   (E) jeopardy

---

comatose stupor

combine unite, blend

commandeer seize for military use

commemorate observe

commend praise

commensurate proportionate

commiserate empathize

commissary food store

commission authorization to perform a task

commodious spacious

commodity product

commodore naval officer

communion fellowship

commutation exchange, substitution

commute lessen punishment

compact covenant

compassion kindness

compatible well-matched, harmonious

compatriot countryman

compelling convincing, persuasive

compendium summary

compensate make up for

compensatory redeeming

competence skillfulness

compile collect

complacent self-satisfied, oblivious to coming danger

compliant submissive, conforming

complicity guilt by association

comport to conduct oneself

composed cool, self-possessed

compound augment

comprehensive thorough

comprise consist of

compulsive obsessive

compulsory obligatory

compunction remorse

concatenate link

concave curving inward

concede yield, grant

concerted done together, intensive effort

conch spiral shell

conciliatory reconciling, restoring goodwill

concise brief

conclusive convincing, ending doubt

concoct devise

concomitant accompanying, concurrent

concord accord

concordat agreement

concourse throng, open space for a gathering

concubine mistress

concur agree

concurrent simultaneous

condescend patronize, talk down to

condiment seasoning

condolence commiseration

condone overlook wrong doing, pardon

conducive helping

conduit pipe

confabulate discuss, give a fictitious account of a past event

confection candy

confederacy alliance

confer bestow

conference meeting

confidant trusted friend

confide trust another (with secrets)

confiscate seize

conflagration large fire

confluence flowing together

confound bewilder

confront challenge

confuse perplex

confute disprove

congeal solidify

congenial friendly

congenital inborn, existing from birth

congeries pile

congruence conformity

coniferous bearing cones

conjecture hypothesis, speculation

conjugal pertaining to marriage

conjure summon

connive conspire

connoisseur an expert, gourmet

consanguineous related by blood

conscientious honorable, upright

conscription draft, enlistment

consecrate make holy

consecutive one after another

consensus general agreement

considered well thought-out, contemplated

consign assign

consolation comfort, solace

console comfort

consolidate unite, strengthen

consonant harmonious

consort spouse

consortium cartel

conspicuous obvious

conspire plot

constellation arrangement of stars

consternation anxiety, bewilderment

constrained confined

construe interpret

consummate perfect

contagion infectious agent

contemplate meditate

contempt disdain

contend struggle

contented satisfied

contentious argumentative

contiguous adjacent, abutting

continence self-control

contingent conditional

contort twist

contraband illicit goods

contraction shrinkage

contractual related to a contract

contrariety opposition

contrast difference, comparison

contravene oppose

contretemps unfortunate occurrence

contrite apologetic

contrive arrange, artificial

controversial subject to dispute

controvert dispute

contumacy disobedience

contusion bruise

Quiz 7 (Matching)

Match each word in the first column with its definition in the second column. Answers are on page 101.

1.	COMMANDEER	A.	seize for military use
2.	COMMUNION	B.	apologetic
3.	COMPATRIOT	C.	perfect
4.	CONCERTED	D.	accord
5.	CONCORD	E.	done together
6.	CONFLUENCE	F.	pile
7.	CONGERIES	G.	flowing together
8.	CONSONANT	H.	harmonious
9.	CONSUMMATE	I.	countryman
10.	CONTRITE	J.	fellowship

conundrum puzzle, enigma

convene assemble (a group)

conventional customary, standard

converge come together

conversant familiar

converse opposite

convex curving outward

convey communicate

conviction strongly held belief

convivial sociable, festive

convocation gathering

convoke convene, summon

convoluted twisted, complicated

copious abundant

coquette a flirt

cordial friendly

cordon bond, chain, barrier

cornucopia cone-shaped horn filled with fruit

corollary consequence

coronation crowning of a sovereign

corporeal of the body

corps group of people

corpulent fat

corroborate confirm

cortege procession

coruscate sparkle

cosmopolitan worldly, sophisticated

cosset coddle

coterie small group

countenance facial expression

countermand overrule

counterstrike strike back

countervail counterbalance

coup master stroke, sudden takeover

coup de grâce final stroke, a blow of mercy

court-martial military trial

courtesan prostitute

courtier member of the king's court

covenant agreement, pact

covert secret

covet desire

cower showing fear

crass crude

crave desire

craven cowardly

credence belief

credenza buffet

credulity gullibility

credulous believing

creed belief

crescendo becoming louder

crestfallen dejected

crevice crack

cringe cower

criterion a standard used in judging

critique examination, criticism

croon sing

cruet bottle

crux gist, key

cryptic mysterious, puzzling

cubism a style of painting

cudgel club

culinary pertaining to cooking

cull pick out, select

culminate climax

culpable blameworthy

culprit offender

culvert drain

cumbersome unwieldy

cumulative accumulate

cupidity greed

curb restrain, block

curmudgeon boor, bad-tempered

curriculum course of study

curry seek favor by flattery

cursory hasty

curt abrupt, rude

curtail shorten

cyclone storm

cynical scornful of the motives or sincerity of others

cynosure celebrity, center of attention

czar Russian emperor

D

dab touch lightly

dais platform

dally procrastinate, linger

dank cold and damp

dauntless courageous

de facto actual, in effect

de jure legally

de rigueur very formal, compulsory

deadpan expressionless

dearth scarcity

debacle a rout, defeat

debase degrade

debauch corrupt

Quiz 8 (Antonyms)

<u>Directions:</u> Choose the word most opposite in meaning to the capitalized word. Answers are on page 101.

1. UPSHOT: (A) consequence (B) descent (C) annihilation (D) termination (E) inception

2. WHET: (A) obscure (B) blunt (C) desiccate (D) imbibe (E) enervate

3. PRODIGY: (A) vacuous comment (B) hegemony (C) plane (D) common occurrence (E) capitulation

4. AMBULATORY: (A) immutable (B) obdurate (C) hospitalized (D) pedantic (E) stationary

5. PLATITUDE: (A) sincere comment (B) enigmatic comment (C) hostile comment (D) disingenuous comment (E) original comment

6. SEEMLY: (A) redoubtable (B) flaccid (C) imperceptible (D) indigenous (E) unbecoming

7. CHAMPION: (A) relinquish (B) contest (C) oppress (D) modify (E) withhold

8. AIR: (A) release (B) differ (C) expose (D) betray (E) enshroud

9. PERTURBATION: (A) impotence (B) obstruction (C) prediction (D) equanimity (E) chivalry

10: TEMPESTUOUS: (A) prodigal (B) reticent (C) serene (D) phenomenal (E) accountable

debauchery indulgence

debilitate weaken

debonair sophisticated, affable

debrief interrogate, inform

debunk refute, expose

debutante a girl debuting into society

decadence decay (e.g. moral or cultural)

decant pour

decapitate kill by beheading

decathlon athletic contest

deceive trick

deciduous shedding leaves

decimate destroy

decipher decode

decline decrease in number

decommission take a ship out of service

decorous seemly, dignified

decorum protocol, etiquette

decree official order

decrepitude enfeeblement

decry castigate

deduce conclude

deduct subtract

deem judge

deface mar, disfigure

defamation (noun) slander

defame (verb) slander

defeatist one who is resigned to defeat

defer postpone

deference courteously yielding to another

deficit shortage

defile pollute, corrupt

definitive conclusive, final

deflect turn aside

deflower despoil

defraud swindle

defray pay

deft skillful

defunct extinct

degrade demean

dehydrate dry out

deign condescend

deity a god

delectable delicious

delegate authorize

delete remove

deleterious harmful

deliberate ponder

delineate draw a line around, describe

delinquent negligent, culpable

delirium mental confusion, ecstasy

delude deceive

deluge a flood

delve dig, explore (of ideas)

demagogue a politician who appeals to base instincts

demean degrade

demeanor behavior

demented deranged

demise death

demobilize disband

demography study of human populations

demoralize dishearten

demote lower in rank

demur take (mild) exception, balk

demure sedate, reserved

denigrate defame

denizen dweller

denomination class, sect

denote signify, stand for

denouement resolution

denounce condemn

denude strip bare

depart leave

depict portray

deplete exhaust

deplore condemn

deploy arrange forces

deportment behavior, posture

deposition testimony

depravity immorality, wickedness

deprecate belittle

depredation preying on, plunder

deprive take away

deracinate uproot

derelict negligent

deride ridicule

derisive mocking

derogatory degrading

derrick crane

desecrate profane, defile

desiccate dehydrate

designate appoint

desist stop

desolate forsaken

despicable contemptible

despise loathe

despondent depressed

despot tyrant

destitute poor

desuetude disuse

desultory without direction in life

detached emotionally removed

detain confine

détente truce

detention confinement

deter discourage, prevent

deterrent hindrance, disincentive

detract lessen, undermine

detractor one who criticizes

detrimental harmful

detritus debris

devastate lay waste

deviate turn away from

devise plan

devoid empty

devotee enthusiast, follower

devout pious

diabolical devilish

dialectic pertaining to debate

diaphanous sheer, translucent

diatribe long denunciation

dicey risky

dichotomy a division into two parts

dictate command

dictum saying

didactic instructional

diffident shy

digress ramble

Quiz 9 (Matching)

Match each word in the first column with its definition in the second column.
Answers are on page 101.

1.	DEBUNK	A.	decode
2.	DECIPHER	B.	refute
3.	DEDUCE	C.	conclusive
4.	DEFINITIVE	D.	conclude
5.	DEFUNCT	E.	to draw a line around
6.	DELINEATE	F.	extinct
7.	DENOMINATION	G.	belittle
8.	DEPRECATE	H.	sect
9.	DESOLATE	I.	pertaining to debate
10.	DIALECTIC	J.	forsaken

dilapidated neglected

dilate enlarge

dilatory procrastinating

dilemma a difficult choice

dilettante amateur, dabbler

diligent hard-working

diminution reduction

diocese district

dire dreadful

dirigible airship, blimp

disabuse correct

disaffect alienate

disarray disorder

disavow deny, disown

disband disperse

disburse pay out

discernible visible

discerning observant

disclaim renounce

disconcert confuse

disconsolate inconsolable

discord lack of harmony

discourse conversation

discreet prudent

discrepancy difference, disagreement

discrete separate

discretion prudence, the ability to make well-reasoned decisions

discriminating able to see differences

discursive rambling

disdain contempt

disengage release, detach

disfigure mar, ruin

disgruntled disappointed

dishevel muss

disinclination unwillingness

disingenuous deceptive, insincere

disinter unearth

disinterested impartial

disjointed disconnected, incoherent

dismal gloomy

dismantle take apart

dismay dread

disparage belittle

disparate various

disparity difference, inequality

dispassionate impartial

dispatch send

dispel cause to banish

disperse scatter

dispirit discourage

disposition attitude, temper

dispossess take away possessions

disputatious fond of arguing

dispute debate

disquietude anxiety

disquisition elaborate treatise

disrepute disgrace

dissemble pretend, hide true beliefs

disseminate distribute

dissent disagree with the majority

dissertation lecture

dissidence disagreement

dissipate scatter, squander

dissolute profligate, immoral

dissolution disintegration

dissonance discord

dissuade deter

distend swell

distortion misinterpret, lie

distract divert

distrait preoccupied, absent-minded

distraught distressed

distrust suspect

dither move without purpose

diurnal daily

diva prima donna

diverge branch off

diverse varying

diversion pastime

diversity variety

divest strip, deprive

dividend distributed profits

divine foretell

divisive causing conflict

divulge disclose

docile domesticated, trained

dock curtail

doctrinaire dogmatic

document verify

dodder tremble

dogged persistent

doggerel poor verse

dogmatic certain, unchanging in opinion

dolce sweetly and gently

doldrums dullness

doleful sorrowful

Quiz 10 (Antonyms)

Directions: Choose the word most opposite in meaning to the capitalized word. Answers are on page 101.

1. CURB: (A) bridle   (B) encourage   (C) reproach
                (D) ameliorate   (E) perjure

2. DOCUMENT: (A) copy   (B) implement   (C) gainsay
                (D) blanch   (E) rant

3. FLUID: (A) radiant   (B) smooth   (C) solid
                (D) balky   (E) craggy

4. BOLT: (A) linger   (B) refrain from   (C) subdue
                (D) strip   (E) transgress

5. TABLE: (A) palliate   (B) acclimate   (C) garner
                (D) propound   (E) expedite

6. HARBOR: (A) provide shelter   (B) banish   (C) acquiesce
                (D) extol   (E) capitulate

7. DISREPUTE: (A) impertinence   (B) indifference   (C) honor
                (D) affluence   (E) apathy

8. STEEP: (A) desiccate   (B) intensify   (C) pontificate
                (D) whet   (E) hamper

9. RENT: (A) reserved   (B) restored   (C) razed
                (D) busy   (E) kinetic

10. EXACT: (A) extract   (B) starve   (C) lecture
                (D) menace   (E) condone

dolorous gloomy

domicile home

dominion area of authority

don assume, put on

donor contributor

dormant asleep

dossier file

dotage senility

doting attending

double-entendre having two meanings one of which is sexually suggestive

doughty resolute, unafraid

dour sullen

dowager widow

doyen dean of a group

draconian harsh

dregs residue, riffraff

drivel inane speech

droll amusing

drone speak in a monotonic voice

dubious doubtful

ductile stretchable

dudgeon resentment, indignant humor

duenna governess

duet twosome

dulcet melodious

dupe one who is easily trick, victim

duplicity deceit, treachery

duress coercion

dynamic energetic

E

ebb recede

ebullient exuberant

eccentric odd, weird

ecclesiastical churchly

echelon degree, rank

éclat brilliance

eclectic from many sources

ectoderm top layer of skin

ecumenical universal, promoting unity

edict order

edifice building

edify instruct

editorialize express an opinion

educe draw forth, evoke

efface obliterate

effeminate unmanly

effervescence exuberance

effete worn out

efficacious effective

efficacy effectiveness

effigy likeness, mannequin

effloresce to bloom

effrontery insolence

effulgent brilliant

effusion pouring forth

egocentric self-centered

egregious grossly wrong

egress exit

ejaculate exclaim

eke supplement with great effort, strain

elaboration detailed explanation

elate raise spirits

electorate voters

eleemosynary pertaining to charity

elegant refined, exquisite

elegiac sad

elephantine large

elicit provoke

elide omit

elite upper-class

ellipsis omission of words

eloquent well-spoken

elucidate make clear, explain

elude evade

elusive evasive

emaciated underfed, gaunt

emancipate liberate

emasculate castrate, dispirit

embargo restriction

embellish exaggerate, adorn

embezzlement theft

emblazon imprint, brand

embody personify

embrace accept, adopt

embrangle embroil

embroil involve with trouble

embryonic rudimentary, nascent

emend correct

emergent appearing

emeritus retired, but retaining title

eminent distinguished, famous

emissary messenger

emote to display exaggerated emotion

empathy compassion, sympathy

employ make use of

empower enable, grant

emulate imitate

enact decree, ordain

enamored charmed, captivated

enate related on the mother's side

encapsulate condense

enchant charm

enclave area enclosed within another region

encomium praise

encompass contain, encircle

encore additional performance

encroach trespass

encumber burden

encyclopedic comprehensive

endear enamor

endeavor attempt, strive

endemic peculiar to a particular region

endocrinologist one who studies glands of internal secretion

endoderm within the skin

endorse approve

endowment property, gift

endure to suffer without giving up

enervate weaken

enfranchise liberate, grant the right to vote

engaging enchanting, charming

engender generate, prompt

engrave carve into a material

engross captivate

engulf overwhelm

enhance improve

enigmatic puzzling

enjoin urge, order, forbid

enlighten inform

enlist join

enmity hostility, hatred

ennoble exalt

ennui boredom, world-weariness

Quiz 11 (Matching)

Match each word in the first column with its definition in the second column. Answers are on page 101.

1.	DORMANT	A.	exuberant
2.	DOUGHTY	B.	puzzling
3.	DUET	C.	comprehensive
4.	EBULLIENT	D.	asleep
5.	EFFEMINATE	E.	omission of words
6.	ELLIPSIS	F.	unmanly
7.	EMANCIPATE	G.	charm
8.	ENCHANT	H.	liberate
9.	ENCYCLOPEDIC	I.	twosome
10.	ENIGMATIC	J.	resolute

enormity large, tragic

ensemble musical group

enshroud cover, obscure

ensnare trap, lure

ensue follow immediately

entail involve, necessitate

enterprise undertaking

enthrall mesmerize

entice lure

entomology the study of insects

entourage assemblage, staff

entreat plead

entrench fortify

entrepreneur businessman

enumerate count

enviable desirable

envision imagine, visualize

envoy messenger

eon long period of time

ephemeral short-lived

epic majestic, a long narrative poem

epicure gourmet

epidemic spreading rapidly

epidemiology study of the spread of disease

epigram saying

episode incident

epistemology the branch of philosophy dealing with knowledge

epithet name, appellation

epoch era

epoxy glue

equable even-tempered

equanimity composure, poise

equine pertaining to horses

equitable fair

equivocate make intentionally ambiguous

era period of time

eradicate abolish

ergo therefore

erode wear away

err mistake, misjudge

errant wandering

erratic constantly changing

erroneous mistaken

ersatz artificial

erudite learned

erupt burst forth

escalate intensify

escapade adventure

escarpment a steep slope

eschew avoid

esoteric known by only a few

esplanade boardwalk

espouse advocate

esteem respect

esthetic artistic

estimable meritorious

estrange alienate

eternal endless

ethereal light, airy

ethical conforming to accepted standards of behavior

ethos beliefs of a group

etiquette manners

etymology study of words

euphemism genteel expression

euphoria elation

euthanasia mercy-killing

evade avoid

evanescent fleeting, very brief

evangelical proselytizing

evasive elusive

eventful momentous

eventual ultimate, coming

eventuate bring about

evidential pertaining to evidence

evince attest, demonstrate

eviscerate disembowel

evoke draw forth

evolution gradual change

ewe female sheep

ex officio by virtue of position

exacerbate worsen

exact use authority to force payment

exacting demanding, difficult

exalt glorify

exasperate irritate

excerpt selection, extract

excision removal

exclaim shout

exclude shut out

exclusive prohibitive

excommunicate expel

excruciate torture

execrable abominable

execute put into effect

exegesis interpretation

Quiz 12 (Antonyms)

Directions: Choose the word most opposite in meaning to the capitalized word. Answers are on page 101.

1. DISCORD: (A) agreement   (B) supposition   (C) strife
    (D) scrutiny   (E) antithesis

2. KEEN: (A) concentrated   (B) languid   (C) rash
    (D) caustic   (E) voracious

3. IRRELEVANT: (A) moot   (B) onerous   (C) impertinent
    (D) germane   (E) true

4. FACILITATE: (A) appease   (B) expedite   (C) extol
    (D) foil   (E) precipitate

5. FEND: (A) absorb   (B) disperse   (C) intensify
    (D) reflect   (E) halt

6. PORTLY: (A) ill   (B) thin   (C) dull
    (D) rotund   (E) insipid

7. DEPLETE: (A) tax   (B) annotate   (C) replenish
    (D) lecture   (E) vanquish

8. INCESSANT: (A) intermittent   (B) continual   (C) increasing
    (D) enclosing   (E) expanding

9. PERJURE: (A) absolve   (B) forswear   (C) impeach
    (D) authenticate   (E) mortify

10. PLETHORA: (A) dishonor   (B) paucity   (C) glut
    (D) resolve   (E) deluge

exemplary outstanding

exempt excuse

exhaustive thorough

exhibitionist one who draws attention to himself

exhort strongly urge

exhume uncover

exigency urgency

exiguous scanty

exile banish

exodus departure, migration

exonerate free from blame

exorbitant expensive

exorcise expel

expanse extent of land

expansive sweeping

expedient advantageous

expedite hasten

expel drive out

expertise knowledge, ability

expiate atone

expletive curse, invective

expliate atone

explicate explain

explicit definite, clear

exploit utilize, milk

expose divulge, reveal

expostulate protest

expound explain

expropriate dispossess, confiscate

expunge erase

exquisite beautifully made

extant existing

extemporize improvise

extent scope

extenuate mitigate

extirpate seek out and destroy

extol praise highly

extort obtain under duress

extract to pull out, exact

extradite deport, deliver

extraneous not essential

extrapolate infer

extremity farthest point, boundary

extricate disentangle

extroverted outgoing

extrude force out

exuberant joyous

exude emit

exult rejoice

F

fabrication a lie

facade mask, front of a building

facet aspect

facetious joking, sarcastic

facile easy

facilitate make easier

facility skill

facsimile duplicate

faction clique, sect

factious causing disagreement

factitious artificial

factotum handyman

fallacious false

fallacy false belief

fallow unproductive, unplowed

falsetto high male voice

falter waver

fanaticism excessive zeal

fane temple

fanfare publicity

farcical absurd, ridiculous

farrago mixture

fascism totalitarianism, extreme nationalism

fastidious meticulous

fatal resulting in death

fathom understand

fatuity foolishness

fatuous inane, stupid

fauna animals

faux pas false step, mistake

fealty loyalty

feasible likely to succeed

feat deed, remarkable achievement

febrile feverish, delirious

feckless incompetent

fecund fertile

feign pretend

felicity happiness

felonious criminal

femme fatale a woman who leads men to their destruction

fend ward off

feral untamed, wild

ferment turmoil

ferret rummage through

fertile fruitful

fervor intensity

fester decay, to make someone increasingly bitter

festive joyous

festoon decorate

fete to honor with an event

fetid stinking

fetters shackles

fey eccentric, whimsical

fiasco debacle

fiat decree

fickle always changing one's mind

fictitious invented, imaginary

fidelity loyalty

figment falsehood, fantasy

filch steal

filial son

filibuster long speech

fillip stimulus

finale conclusion

finesse skill

firebrand agitator

firmament sky

fiscal monetary

fitful starting and stopping irregularly

fjord coastal inlet

flabbergasted amazed, bumdfounded

flagellate whip

flagrant outrageous, blatant

flail whip, to thrash something around uncontrollably and menacingly

fledgling just beginning, struggling

flippant pert, glib, dismissive

florid ruddy, ornate

Quiz 13 (Matching)

Match each word in the first column with its definition in the second column. Answers are on page 101.

1.	EXHORT	A.	free from blame
2.	EXONERATE	B.	strongly urge
3.	EXPOSTULATE	C.	agitator
4.	EXTRADITE	D.	untamed
5.	EXULT	E.	debacle
6.	FACTITIOUS	F.	inane
7.	FATUOUS	G.	artificial
8.	FERAL	H.	deport
9.	FIASCO	I.	rejoice
10.	FIREBRAND	J.	protest

flout to show disregard for the law or rules

fluctuate waver, vary

foible weakness, minor fault

foil defeat, thwart

foist palm off a fake

foment instigate

font source, fountainhead, set of type

forage search for food

foray raid

forbear abstain, restrain oneself

force majeure superior force

foreboding ominous

foreclose exclude

forensic pertaining to debate

foresight ability to predict the future

forestall thwart, preempt

forgo relinquish (usually voluntarily)

forsake abandon

forswear deny

forthright frank

forthwith immediately

fortify strengthen

fortitude resilience, courage

fortuitous lucky

foster encourage, cultivate

founder sink. fail

fracas noisy fight

fragile easily broken

fragmented broken into fragments

fraternity brotherhood

fraught filled

frenetic harried, neurotic

fret worry

fritter squander

frivolity playfulness

frolic romp, play

frond bending tree

frugal thrifty

fruitful productive

fruition realization, completion

fruitless unprofitable, barren

fulminate denounce, menace

fulsome excessive, insincere

fuming angry

furlough leave of absence

furor commotion

furtive stealthy

fusillade bombardment

futile hopeless

G

gaffe embarrassing mistake

gainful profitable

gainsay contradict

galvanize excite to action

gambit plot, strategy

gamut range, scope

gargantuan large

garner gather

garnish decorate

garrote stranglehold

garrulous talkative

gauche awkward

genealogy ancestry

generic general

genesis beginning

genetics study of heredity

genre kind, category

genteel elegant, refined

genuflect kneel in reverence

genuine authentic, sincere

geriatrics pertaining to old age

germane relevant

ghastly horrible

gibe heckle

gingivitis inflammation of the gums

gist essence (of an argument)

glabrous without hair

glaucoma disorder of the eye

glean gather

glib insincere manner

glower stare angrily

glut surplus, excess

glutton one who eats too much

gnarl deform

gnome dwarf-like being

goad encourage, provoke

googol a very large number

gorge stuff, satiate

gorgon ugly person

gormandize eat voraciously

gory bloody

gossamer thin and flimsy

Gothic medieval style of architecture

gouge overcharge

gracious kindness, politeness

gradient incline, rising by degrees

Quiz 14 (Antonyms)

Directions: Choose the word most opposite in meaning to the capitalized word. Answers are on page 101.

1. ASSIMILATE: (A) strive   (B) adapt   (C) synchronize
    (D) estrange   (E) officiate

2. INADVERTENT: (A) accidental   (B) disingenuous   (C) forthright
    (D) inconsiderate   (E) calculated

3. ABSCOND: (A) pilfer   (B) replace   (C) glean
    (D) substitute   (E) surrender

4. FOMENT: (A) exhort   (B) dissuade   (C) cower
    (D) abet   (E) fixate

5. EXTENUATE: (A) alleviate   (B) preclude   (C) worsen
    (D) subdue   (E) justify

6. NONPAREIL: (A) consummate   (B) juvenile   (C) dutiful
    (D) ordinary   (E) choice

7. REPUDIATE: (A) denounce   (B) deceive   (C) embrace
    (D) fib   (E) generalize

8. NOXIOUS: (A) diffuse   (B) latent   (C) beneficial
    (D) unique   (E) unjust

9. SUFFRAGE: (A) absence of charity   (B) absence of franchise
    (C) absence of pain   (D) absence of success
    (E) absence of malice

10. GLEAN: (A) gaffe   (B) furor   (C) gather
    (D) frolic   (E) foist

gradual by degrees, changing slowly

grandiose impressive, large

granular grainy

grapple struggle

gratis free

gratitude thankfulness

gratuitous unwarranted, uncalled for

gratuity tip

gravamen the essential part of an accusation

gravity seriousness

gregarious sociable

grievous tragic, heinous

grimace expression of disgust or pain

grisly gruesome

grovel crawl, obey, beg

grudging reluctant

guffaw laughter

guile deceit

gullible easily deceived

gusto great enjoyment

guttural throaty

gyrate whirl

H

habitat natural environment

habituate accustom

hackneyed trite

haggard gaunt

halcyon serene

hale healthy

hallucination delusion

hamper obstruct

hapless unlucky

harangue tirade

harass torment

harbinger forerunner

harbor give shelter, conceal

hardy healthy

harlequin clown

harp complain incessantly

harridan hag

harrowing distressing

harry harass

haughty arrogant

haven refuge

havoc destruction, chaos

hearsay gossip

hedonism the pursuit of pleasure in life

heed follow advice

heedless careless

hegemony authority, domination

hegira a journey to a more pleasant place

heinous vile, atrocious

heliocentric having the sun as a center

helix a spiral

helots slaves

herald harbinger

herbivorous feeding on plants

Herculean powerful, large

hermetic airtight, sealed

hermit one who lives in solitude

herpetologist one who studies reptiles

heterodox departing form established doctrines

heuristic teaching device or method

hew cut

heyday glory days, prime

hiatus interruption

hibernal wintry

hidalgo nobleman

hidebound prejudiced, provincial

hideous horrible

hie to hasten

highbrow intellectual

hirsute bearded

histrionic overly dramatic

holograph written entirely by hand

homage respect

homely plain

homily sermon

homogeneous uniform

homonym words that are identical in spelling and pronunciation

hone sharpen

horde group

hortatory inspiring good deeds

hospice shelter

hovel shanty, cabin

hoyden tomboy

hubris arrogance

hue color

humane compassionate

humanities languages and literature

humility humbleness

hummock knoll, mound

humus soil

husbandry management

hybrid crossbreed

hydrophobia fear of water

hygienic sanitary

hymeneal pertaining to marriage

hymn religious song

hyperactive overactive

hyperbole exaggeration

hypertension elevated blood pressure

hypocritical deceiving, two-faced

hypoglycemic low blood sugar

hypothermia low body temperature

I

ibidem in the same place

ichthyology study of fish

iconoclast one who rails against sacred institutions

idiosyncrasy peculiarity

idyllic natural, picturesque

ignoble dishonorable

ilk class, clan

illicit unlawful

illimitable limitless

illusory fleeting, deceptive

illustrious famous

imbibe drink

imbue infuse

immaculate spotlessly clean

immaterial irrelevant

immense huge

Quiz 15 (Matching)

Match each word in the first column with its definition in the second column. Answers are on page 101.

1.	GRANDIOSE	A.	drink
2.	GRIEVOUS	B.	pertaining to marriage
3.	HALCYON	C.	arrogance
4.	HARLEQUIN	D.	prejudiced
5.	HEDONISM	E.	teaching device or method
6.	HEURISTIC	F.	the pursuit of pleasure in life
7.	HIDEBOUND	G.	clown
8.	HUBRIS	H.	serene
9.	HYMENEAL	I.	heinous
10.	IMBIBE	J.	impressive

immerse bathe, engross

imminent about to happen

immobile still

immolate sacrifice (especially by fire)

immunity exemption from prosecution

immure build a wall around

immutable unchangeable, absolute

impair injure

impale pierce

impartial not biased

impasse deadlock

impassioned fiery, emotional

impassive calm

impeach accuse, charge

impeccable faultless

impecunious indigent

impede hinder

impediment obstacle

impel urge, force

impending approaching, imminent

imperative vital, pressing

imperceptible slight, intangible

imperialism colonialism

imperil endanger

imperious domineering

impertinent insolent

imperturbable calm, unflappable

impervious impenetrable, unreceptive

impetuous impulsive

impetus stimulus, spark

impinge encroach, touch

implant instill

implausible unlikely, improbable

implement carry out, execute

implicate incriminate

implicit implied

implore entreat

implosion bursting inward

impolitic unwise, inappropriate

imponderable difficult to estimate

import meaning, significance

importune urgent request

imposing intimidating, stately

imposition intrusion, burden

impotent powerless

impound seize

imprecation curse, inculcate

impregnable invincible

impresario promoter

impressionable susceptible, easily influenced

impressionism a style of painting

imprimatur sanction

impromptu spontaneous

improvise invent

impudence insolence

impugn criticize, accuse

impulse inclination, sudden desire

impulsive to act suddenly

impunity exemption from harm

impute charge

in toto in full, entirely

inadvertent unintentional

inadvisable not recommended

inalienable that which cannot be taken away

inane vacuous, stupid

inanimate inorganic, lifeless

inaudible cannot be heard

inaugurate induct (with a ceremony)

inborn innate

incalculable immeasurable

incandescent brilliant

incantation chant

incapacitate disable

incarcerate imprison

incarnate embody, personify

incendiary inflammatory

incense enrage

incentive stimulus, inducement

incessant unceasing

incest sex among family members

inchoate just begun

incidental insignificant, minor

incinerate burn

incipient beginning

incision cut

incisive keen, penetrating

incite foment, provoke

incivility rudeness

inclement harsh, stormy

inclusive comprehensive

incognito disguised

incommunicado unable to communicate with others

incomparable peerless

incompatibility inability to live in harmony

Quiz 16 (Analogies)

<u>Directions:</u> Choose the pair that expresses a relationship most similar to that expressed in the capitalized pair. Answers are on page 101.

1. ANARCHY : GOVERNMENT ::
   - (A) confederation : state
   - (B) trepidation : courage
   - (C) serenity : equanimity
   - (D) surfeit : food
   - (E) computer : hard drive

2. Galvanize : Charismatic Leader ::
   - (A) jeer : fan
   - (B) correct : charlatan
   - (C) impeach : President
   - (D) retreat : champion
   - (E) moderate : arbiter

3. PARRY : BLOW ::
   - (A) equivocate : question
   - (B) cower : start
   - (C) boomerang : backlash
   - (D) cast : invective
   - (E) browbeat : chastity

4. DISQUIETUDE : ANXIOUS ::
   - (A) magnitude : unabridged
   - (B) isolation : sequestered
   - (C) cupidity : bellicose
   - (D) embellishment : overstated
   - (E) nonplus : perplexed

5. MILK : DRAIN ::
   - (A) insult : commend
   - (B) abstract : distend
   - (C) extend : disregard
   - (D) exploit : employ
   - (E) assail : rescind

6. ABSTRUSE : CLEAR ::
   - (A) nondescript : conspicuous
   - (B) high-brow : indifferent
   - (C) affable : agreeable
   - (D) prominent : manifest
   - (E) complex : hard

7. OMNISCIENT : KNOWLEDGE ::
   - (A) saturnine : energy
   - (B) complete : retraction
   - (C) principled : method
   - (D) inquisitive : science
   - (E) boundless : expanse

8. STOKE : SMOTHER ::
   - (A) incinerate : heat
   - (B) animate : enervate
   - (C) contest : decry
   - (D) acknowledge : apprehend
   - (E) garrote : asphyxiate

9. ORCHESTRA : MUSICIAN ::
   - (A) story : comedian
   - (B) band : singer
   - (C) garden : leaf
   - (D) troupe : actor
   - (E) government : lawyer

10. MUTTER : INDISTINCT ::
   - (A) define : easy
   - (B) blunder : polished
   - (C) articulate : well-spoken
   - (D) expedite : completed
   - (E) censure : histrionic

inconceivable unthinkable

incongruous out of place, absurd

inconsiderate thoughtless, insensitive

inconspicuous not noticeable

incontrovertible indisputable

incorporate combine

incorrigible unreformable

incredulous skeptical

increment step, increase

incriminate accuse

incubus nightmare

inculcate instill, indoctrinate

inculpate accuse

incumbent obligatory

incursion raid

indecent offensive, lewd

indecorous unseemly

indelible permanent

indemnity insurance

indict charge

indifferent unconcerned

indigenous native

indigent poor

indignant resentment of injustice

indiscreet lacking sound judgment, rash

indiscriminate random

indispensable vital, essential

indistinct blurry, without clear features

indolent lazy

indomitable invincible

indubitable unquestionable

induce persuade, provoke

indulge succumb to desire

indurate harden

industrious hard-working

inebriate intoxicate

ineffable inexpressible

ineffectual futile

ineluctable inescapable

inept unfit, incompetent

inert inactive

inestimable priceless, immeasurable

inevitable unavoidable, predestined

inexorable relentless

infallible unerring

infamous notorious

infamy shame

infantry foot soldiers

infatuate immature love

infer conclude

infernal hellish

infidel nonbeliever

infidelity disloyalty

infiltrate trespass

infinitesimal very small

infirmary clinic

infirmity ailment

inflammatory incendiary

influx inflow

infraction violation

infringe encroach

infuriate enrage

infuse inspire, instill

ingenious clever, resourceful

ingrate ungrateful person

ingratiate pleasing, flattering, endearing

ingress entering

inherent innate, inborn

inhibit restrain

inimical adverse, hostile

inimitable peerless

iniquitous unjust, wicked

iniquity sin, injustice

initiate begin

initiation induction ceremony

injunction command

inkling hint

innate inborn

innervate invigorate

innocuous harmless

innovative new, useful idea

innuendo insinuation

inopportune untimely

inordinate excessive

inquest investigation

inquisition interrogation

inquisitive curious

insatiable gluttonous

inscribe engrave

inscrutable cannot be fully understood

insensate without feeling

insidious treacherous, sinister

insignia emblems

insinuate allude

insipid flat, dull

insolent insulting

insolvent bankrupt

insouciant nonchalant

installment portion, payment

instant at once

instigate incite

insubordinate disobedient

insufferable unbearable

insular narrow-minded

insuperable insurmountable

insurgent rebellious

insurrection uprising

intangible not perceptible by touch

integral essential

integrate make whole

integration unification

integument a covering

intelligentsia the intellectual elite of society

intensive extreme, concentrated

inter bury

intercede plead on behalf of another

intercept prevent, cut off

interdict prohibit

interject interrupt

Quiz 17 (Matching)

Match each word in the first column with its definition in the second column.
Answers are on page 101.

1.	INCONGRUOUS	A.	harden
2.	INCONSPICUOUS	B.	relentless
3.	INDECOROUS	C.	hostile
4.	INDIGNANT	D.	cannot be fully understood
5.	INDURATE	E.	out of place, absurd
6.	INEXORABLE	F.	not noticeable
7.	INIMICAL	G.	unseemly
8.	INSCRUTABLE	H.	resentment of injustice
9.	INSOUCIANT	I.	nonchalant
10.	INSUPERABLE	J.	insurmountable

---

interloper intruder

interlude intermission

interminable unending

internecine mutually destructive

interpolate insert

interpose insert

interregnum interval between two successive reigns

interrogate question

intersperse scatter

interstate between states

intervene interfere, mediate

intestate leaving no will

intimate allude to, hint

intractable unmanageable

intransigent unyielding

intrepid fearless

intricate complex

intrigue plot, mystery

intrinsic inherent

introspection self-analysis

inundate flood

inure accustom, habituate, harden

invalidate disprove, nullify

invective verbal insult

inveigh to rail against

inveigle lure, wheedle

inventive cleaver, resourceful

inverse directly opposite

inveterate habitual, chronic

invidious incurring ill-will

invincible cannot be defeated

inviolate sacred, unchangeable

invocation calling on God

irascible irritable

irate angry

ironic oddly contrary to what is expected

irrational illogical

irrelevant unrelated, immaterial

irreparable cannot be repaired

irresolute hesitant, uncertain

irrevocable cannot be rescinded

isosceles having two equal sides

itinerant wandering

itinerary route

J

jabberwocky nonsense

jaded spent, bored with one's situation

jargon specialized vocabulary

jaundiced biased, embittered

jeer mock

jejune barren, unsophisticated

jest joke

jilt reject, end a relationship promptly

jingoistic nationalistic, warmongering

jocular humorous

jostle push, brush against

journeyman reliable worker

joust combat between knights on horses

jubilant in high spirits

judicious prudent

juggernaut unstoppable force

jugular throat

juncture pivotal point in time

junoesque stately beauty

junta small ruling group

jurisdiction domain

jurisprudence law

justify excuse, mitigate

juvenescent making young, growing out of infancy and into childhood

juxtapose to place side by side

K

kaleidoscope series of changing events

keen of sharp mind

ken purview, range of comprehension

kindle arouse, inspire

kindred similar, related by blood

kinetic pertaining to motion

kismet fate, the will of Allah

kite bad check

kitsch trashy art

kleptomania impulse to steal

knave con man

knead massage, to fold, press, and stretch a substance into a uniform mass

knell sound of a bell

Koran holy book of Islam

kowtow behave obsequiously

kudos acclaim

L

labyrinth maze

lacerate tear, cut

Quiz 18 (Analogies)

Directions: Choose the pair that expresses a relationship most similar to that expressed in the capitalized pair. Answers are on page 101.

1. LOQUACIOUS : GARRULOUS ::

    (A)   harsh : kindly
    (B)   animate : weary
    (C)   gluttonous : disloyal
    (D)   rash : impetuous
    (E)   blithe : gloomy

2. EMPATHY : FEELING ::

    (A)   melancholy : joy
    (B)   sibling : relative
    (C)   Spartan : wickedness
    (D)   boldness : guilt
    (E)   institution : encouragement

3. DEVIATE : LECTURE ::

    (A)   broadcast : information
    (B)   disown : friend
    (C)   welcome: indifference
    (D)   entreat : solicitation
    (E)   meander : drive

4. NEBULOUS : FORM ::

    (A)   insincere : misanthrope
    (B)   benevolent : excellence
    (C)   insipid : taste
    (D)   discerning : hope
    (E)   composed : innocence

5. PENSIVE : MELANCHOLY ::

    (A)   scornful : contempt
    (B)   confident : victory
    (C)   eloquent : optimism
    (D)   sorrowful : indifference
    (E)   contumacious : esteem

6. ANATHEMA : CURSE ::

    (A)   hex : blessing
    (B)   admonition : censure
    (C)   incantation : discernment
    (D)   theory : calculation
    (E)   conjecture : truth

7. DILIGENT : ASSIDUOUS ::

    (A)   suspicious : reliable
    (B)   cautious : indecisive
    (C)   repentant : innocent
    (D)   peerless : common
    (E)   indigent : poor

8. LAMPOON : MOCK::

    (A)   exalt : ennoble
    (B)   entice : disown
    (C)   prattle : talk
    (D)   entreat : controvert
    (E)   debate : heckle

9. INTUITIVE : CONSIDERED ::

    (A)   impromptu : planning
    (B)   laborious : safe
    (C)   ethereal : light
    (D)   random : sequential
    (E)   rational : certain

10. ETERNAL : EPHEMERAL ::

    (A)   equivocal : ambiguous
    (B)   hopeless : chance
    (C)   animated : blithe
    (D)   mysterious : perplexing
    (E)   foreign : familiar

lachrymose tearful

lackey servant

laconic brief, terse

lactic derived from milk

lacuna a missing part, gap

laggard loafer, slacker

lagniappe bonus

laity laymen

lambent softly radiant

lament mourn

lamina layer

lampoon satirize

languish weaken

lanyard short rope

larceny theft

largess generous donation

lascivious lustful

lassitude lethargy

latent potential, dormant

laudatory commendable

laurels fame, success

lave wash

lavish extravagant

lax loose, careless

laxity carelessness

layman nonprofessional

lectern reading desk

leery cautious, doubtful

legacy bequest

legerdemain trickery

legible readable

legislate make laws

legitimate lawful

lenient forgiving

lethargic drowsy, sluggish

levee embankment, dam

leviathan a monster

levity frivolity

liable legally responsible

liaison relationship, affair

libertarian one who believes in complete freedom

libertine roué, rake

libidinous lustful

licentious lewd, immoral

lien financial claim

lieutenant one who acts in place of another

ligature bond

ligneous wood like

Lilliputian very small

limerick poem

limn portray, describe

limpid transparent, clearly understood

linchpin something that is indispensable

lineage ancestry

linguistics study of language

liquidate eliminate

lissome agile, supple

listless lacking spirit or interest

litany list

lithe supple

litigate contest with a lawsuit

litotes two negative statement that cancel to make a positive statement

liturgy ceremony

livid enraged

loath reluctant

loathe abhor, dislike

lofty high

logistics means of supplying troops

logo symbol

logy sluggish

loquacious talkative

lothario rake, womanizer

lout goon, hoodlum

lucid clearly understood

lucrative profitable

lucre money, profit

ludicrous absurd

lugubrious extremely sad

luminous bright

lupine wolf-like

lure entice

lurid ghastly, sensational

luster gloss, sheen

luxuriant lush, lavish

lynch to execute by hanging without a trial

M

macabre gruesome

Machiavellian politically crafty, cunning

machination plot

macrobiosis longevity

macroscopic visibly large

maelstrom whirlpool

magisterial arbitrary, dictatorial

magnanimous generous, kindhearted

magnate a powerful, successful person (especially of business)

magnitude size

magnum opus masterpiece

maim injure, disfigure

maladjusted disturbed

maladroit clumsy

malady illness

malaise uneasiness, weariness

malapropism comical misuse of a word

malcontent one who is forever dissatisfied

malediction curse

malefactor evildoer

malevolence bad intent, malice

malfeasance wrong doing (especially by an official of government)

malice spite

malign defame

malignant virulent, pernicious

malinger shirk

malleable moldable, tractable

Quiz 19 (Matching)

Match each word in the first column with its definition in the second column.
Answers are on page 101.

1.	LACHRYMOSE	A.	trickery
2.	LAGGARD	B.	roué
3.	LASCIVIOUS	C.	very small
4.	LEGERDEMAIN	D.	tearful
5.	LIBERTINE	E.	loafer
6.	LILLIPUTIAN	F.	lustful
7.	LOQUACIOUS	G.	talkative
8.	MACHIAVELLIAN	H.	comical misuse of a word
9.	MAGISTERIAL	I.	arbitrary, dictatorial
10.	MALAPROPISM	J.	politically crafty, cunning

malodorous fetid

mammoth huge

manacle shackle

mandate command

mandatory obligatory

mandrill baboon

mania madness, obsession

manifest obvious, evident

manifesto proclamation

manifold multiple, diverse

manslaughter killing another person without malice

manumit set free

manuscript unpublished book

mar damage

marauder plunderer

marginal insignificant

marionette puppet

maroon abandon

marshal array, mobilize

martial warlike

martinet disciplinarian

martyr sacrifice, symbol

masochist one who enjoys pain

masticate chew

mastiff large dog

mastodon extinct elephant

maternal motherly

maternity motherhood

matriarch matron

matriculate enroll (usually in school)

matrix array

matutinal early, morning

maudlin weepy, sentimental

maul rough up

mausoleum tomb

maverick a rebel, individualist

mawkish sickeningly sentimental

mayhem mutilation, chaos

mea culpa my fault

meager scanty

meander roam, ramble

median middle

mediocre average

medley mixture

megalith ancient stone monument

melancholy reflective, gloomy

melee riot

mellifluous sweet sounding

melodious melodic

memento souvenir

memoir autobiography

memorabilia things worth remembering

memorandum note

menagerie zoo

mendacity untruth

mendicant beggar

menial humble, degrading

mentor teacher

mercantile commercial

mercenary calculating, venal

mercurial changeable, volatile

metamorphosis a change in form

mete distribute

meteoric swift, dazzling

meteorology science of weather

methodical systematic, careful

meticulous extremely careful, precise

metier occupation

metonymy the substitution of a phrase for the name itself

mettle courage, capacity for bravery

miasma toxin fumes

mien appearance, bearing

migrate travel

milieu environment

militant combative, activist

militate work against

milk extract

millennium thousand-year period

minatory threatening

mince chop, moderate

minion subordinate

minstrel troubadour

minuscule small

minute very small

minutiae trivia

mirage illusion

mire marsh, a situation that is difficult to escape from

mirth jollity

misanthrope hater of mankind

misappropriation use dishonestly

misbegotten illegitimate, obtained by dishonest means

miscarry abort

miscegenation intermarriage between races

Quiz 20 (Analogies)

Directions: Choose the pair that expresses a relationship most similar to that expressed in the capitalized pair. Answers are on page 101.

1. SPEECH : FILIBUSTER ::

    (A)   race : marathon
    (B)   gift : breach
    (C)   statement : digression
    (D)   detour : path
    (E)   address : postage

2. ARISTOCRAT : LAND ::

    (A)   bureaucracy : enslavement
    (B)   monarchy : abnegation
    (C)   gentry : talent
    (D)   dignitary : rank
    (E)   junta : anarchy

3. SURREPTITIOUS : STEALTH ::

    (A)   clandestine : openness
    (B)   guarded : effrontery
    (C)   bombastic : irreverence
    (D)   pernicious : bane
    (E)   impertinent : humility

4. PECCADILLO : FLAW ::

    (A)   mediator : dispute
    (B)   grammar : error
    (C)   nick : score
    (D)   forensics : judiciary
    (E)   invasion : putsch

5. LEVEE : RIVER ::

    (A)   rampart : barrier
    (B)   cordon : throng
    (C)   broker : investment
    (D)   promontory : height
    (E)   string : guitar

6. HEDONIST : UNSTINTING ::

    (A)   protagonist : insignificant
    (B)   thug : aggressive
    (C)   politician : irresolute
    (D)   benefactor : generous
    (E)   drunkard : manifest

7. EXCERPT : NOVEL ::

    (A)   critique : play
    (B)   review : manuscript
    (C)   swatch : cloth
    (D)   foreword : preface
    (E)   recital : performance

8. EXORCISM : DEMON ::

    (A)   matriculation : induction
    (B)   banishment : member
    (C)   qualm : angel
    (D)   heuristic : method
    (E)   manifesto : spirit

9. HOPE : CYNICAL ::

    (A)   reticence : benevolent
    (B)   contention : bellicose
    (C)   bliss : sullen
    (D)   homage : industrious
    (E)   unconcern : indifferent

10. Exhibitionist : Attention ::

    (A)   sycophant : turmoil
    (B)   scientist : power
    (C)   megalomaniac : solitude
    (D)   martyr : anonymity
    (E)   mercenary : money

miscellany mixture of items

misconstrue misinterpret

miscreant evildoer

misgiving doubt, hesitation

misnomer wrongly named

misogyny hatred of women

misshapen deformed

missive letter

mitigate lessen the severity

mnemonics that which aids the memory

mobilize assemble for action

mobocracy rule by mob

modicum pittance

modish chic

module unit

mogul powerful person

molest bother, sexually assault

mollify appease

molten melted

momentous of great importance

monocle eyeglass

monolithic large and uniform

monologue long speech

monstrosity distorted, abnormal form

moot disputable, no longer relevant

moral ethical

morale spirit, confidence

morass swamp, difficult situation

moratorium postponement

mordant biting, sarcastic

mores moral standards

moribund near death

morose sullen

morphine painkilling drug

morsel bite, piece

mortify humiliate

mosque temple

mote speck

motif artistic theme

motive reason for doing something

motley diverse

mottled spotted

motto slogan, saying

mountebank charlatan

mousy drab, colorless

muckraker reformer

muffle stifle, quiet

mulct defraud

multifarious diverse, many-sided

multitude throng

mundane ordinary

munificent generous

murmur mutter, mumble

muse ponder

muster to gather one's forces

mutability able to change

mute silent

mutilate maim

mutiny rebellion

mutter murmur, grumble

muzzle restrain, stifle

myopic narrow-minded

myriad innumerable

myrmidons loyal followers

mystique mystery, aura

mythical fictitious

N

nadir lowest point

narcissism self-love

narrate tell, recount

nascent incipient

natal related to birth

nativity the process of birth

naturalize grant citizenship

ne'er-do-well loafer, idler

nebulous indistinct

necromancy sorcery

nefarious evil

negate cancel

negligible insignificant

nemesis implacable foe

neologism newly coined expression

neonatal newborn

neophyte beginner

nepotism favoritism

nervy brash

nether under

nettle irritate

neurotic disturbed

neutralize offset, nullify

nexus a link between two or more people or things

nicety euphemism

niche nook, an activity that well suits a person's talents

niggardly stingy

nimble spry

nirvana bliss, the attainment of spiritual enlightenment

noctambulism sleepwalking

nocturnal pertaining to night

nocturne serenade

noisome harmful, disgusting

nomad wanderer

nomenclature terminology

nominal slight, in name only

nominate propose, recommend somebody for a position

nominee candidate

nonchalant casual

noncommittal neutral, circumspect

nondescript lacking distinctive features

nonentity person of no significance

nonesuch paragon, one in a thousand

nonpareil unequaled, peerless

nonpartisan neutral, uncommitted

nonplus confound, befuddle

notable remarkable, noteworthy

noted famous

notorious wicked, widely known

nouveau riche newly rich

Quiz 21 (Matching)

Match each word in the first column with its definition in the second column.
Answers are on page 101.

1.	MISCELLANY	A.	peerless
2.	MISSIVE	B.	to gather one's forces
3.	MOOT	C.	newly coined expression
4.	MOUNTEBANK	D.	self-love
5.	MULTIFARIOUS	E.	loyal followers
6.	MUSTER	F.	letter
7.	MYRMIDONS	G.	diverse
8.	NARCISSISM	H.	charlatan
9.	NEOLOGISM	I.	disputable
10.	NONPAREIL	J.	mixture of items

nova bright star

novel new, unique

novice beginner

noxious toxic

nuance shade, subtlety

nub crux, crucial point

nubile marriageable

nugatory useless, worthless

nuisance annoyance

nullify void

nullity nothingness

numismatics coin collecting

nurture nourish, foster

nymph goddess

O

oaf awkward person

obdurate unyielding, hardhearted

obeisance homage, deference

obelisk tall column, monument

obese fat

obfuscate bewilder, muddle

obituary eulogy

objective (adj.) unbiased

objective (noun) goal

objectivity impartiality

oblation offering, sacrifice

obligatory required, compulsory

oblige compel

obliging accommodating, considerate

oblique indirect

obliquity perversity

obliterate destroy

oblong elliptical, oval

obloquy slander

obscure vague, unclear

obsequious fawning, servile

obsequy funeral ceremony

observant watchful

obsolete outdated

obstinate stubborn

obstreperous noisy, unruly

obtain gain possession

obtrusive forward, meddlesome

obtuse stupid

obviate make unnecessary

Occident the West

occlude block

occult mystical, secret, relating to the supernatural or witchcraft

octogenarian person in her eighties

ocular optic, visual

ode poem

odious despicable

odoriferous pleasant odor

odyssey journey

offal inedible parts of a butchered animal

offertory church collection

officiate supervise

officious forward, obtrusive

offset counterbalance

ogle flirt

ogre monster, demon

oleaginous oily

oligarchy aristocracy

olio medley

ominous threatening

omnibus collection, compilation

omnipotent all-powerful

omniscient all-knowing

onerous burdensome

onslaught powerful attack

ontology the study of the nature of existence

onus burden

opaque nontransparent

operative working

operetta musical comedy

opiate narcotic

opine think, express an opinion

opportune well-timed, appropriate

oppress persecute

oppressive burdensome

opprobrious abusive, scornful

opprobrium disgrace

oppugn assail

opt decide, choose

optimum best condition

optional elective

opulence wealth

opus literary work or musical composition

oracle prophet

oration speech

orator speaker

orb sphere

orchestrate organize

ordain appoint

Quiz 22 (Analogies)

<u>Directions:</u> Choose the pair that expresses a relationship most similar to that expressed in the capitalized pair. Answers are on page 101.

1. PARAGRAPH : ESSAY ::
   - (A) trailer : automobile
   - (B) query : question
   - (C) instrument : surgery
   - (D) penmanship : essay
   - (E) shot : salvo

2. COMPOUND : BUILDING ::
   - (A) classroom : campus
   - (B) department : government
   - (C) tapestry : fabric
   - (D) seed : vegetable
   - (E) commonwealth : country

3. CONSTELLATION : STARS ::
   - (A) amplifier : hearing
   - (B) ocean : water
   - (C) mosaic : tile
   - (D) tracks : train
   - (E) book : paper

4. ACCELERATE : VELOCITY ::
   - (A) relinquish : assets
   - (B) energize : stamina
   - (C) protect : parent
   - (D) project : futility
   - (E) educate : stupor

5. SIDEREAL : STARS ::
   - (A) platonic : radiation
   - (B) avian : fish
   - (C) corporeal : heaven
   - (D) heliocentric : transportation
   - (E) terrestrial : Earth

6. STATE : CONFEDERACY ::
   - (A) apple : tree
   - (B) return address : envelope
   - (C) binoculars : sight
   - (D) velocity : acceleration
   - (E) soldier : army

7. HELPFUL : OFFICIOUS ::
   - (A) difficult : incorrigible
   - (B) maudlin : sardonic
   - (C) apathetic : zealous
   - (D) true : contrary
   - (E) friendly : amiable

8. SATURATE : DAMPEN ::
   - (A) contaminate : pollute
   - (B) besmirch : sully
   - (C) extol : praise
   - (D) waive : donate
   - (E) pronounce : presume

9. WAYLAY : ADVANCEMENT ::
   - (A) corroborate : testimony
   - (B) amuse : jeopardy
   - (C) condescend : frenzy
   - (D) curb : movement
   - (E) negotiate : defeat

10. MITIGATE : INJURY ::
   - (A) exacerbate : recovery
   - (B) palliate : accusation
   - (C) dampen : enthusiasm
   - (D) darken : obscurity
   - (E) entreat : ultimatum

orderly neat, arranged

ordinance law

ordnance artillery

orient align, familiarize

orison prayer

ornate lavishly decorated

ornithology study of birds

orthodox conventional

oscillate waver, swing

ossify harden

ostensible apparent, seeming

ostentatious pretentious

ostracize banish, shun

otherworldly spiritual

otiose idle

ouster ejection

outmoded out-of-date

outré eccentric

outset beginning

ovation applause

overrule disallow

overture advance, proposal

overweening arrogant, forward

overwhelm overpower

overwrought overworked, high-strung

ovum egg, cell

P

pachyderm elephant

pacifist one who opposes all violence

pacify appease

pact agreement

paean a song of praise

pagan heathen, ungodly

page attendant

pageant exhibition, show

pains great effort, attention to detail

painstaking taking great care, thorough

palatial grand, splendid

palaver babble, nonsense

Paleolithic stone age

paleontologist one who studies fossils

pall to become dull or weary

palliate assuage

pallid pale, sallow

palpable touchable

palpitate beat, throb

palsy paralysis

paltry scarce

pan criticize

panacea cure-all

panache flamboyance

pandemic widespread, plague

pandemonium din, commotion

pander cater to people's baser instincts

panegyric praise

pang short sharp pain

panoply full suit of armor

panorama vista

pant gasp, puff

pantomime mime

pantry storeroom

papyrus paper

parable allegory

paradigm a model

paragon standard of excellence

parameter limit

paramount chief, foremost

paramour lover

paranoid obsessively suspicious, demented

paranormal supernatural

parapet rampart, defense

paraphernalia equipment

paraphrase restatement

parcel package

parchment paper

pare peel

parenthetical in parentheses

pariah outcast

parish fold, church

parity equality

parlance local speech

parlay increase

parley conference

parochial provincial

parody imitation, ridicule

parole release

paroxysm outburst, convulsion

parrot mimic

parry avert, ward off

parsimonious stingy

parson clergyman

partake share, receive, consume

partial incomplete

partiality bias

parting farewell, severance

partisan supporter

partition division

parvenu newcomer, social climber

pasquinade satire

passé outmoded

passim here and there

pastel pale

pasteurize disinfect

pastoral rustic

patent obvious

paternal fatherly

pathetic pitiful

pathogen agent causing disease

pathogenic causing disease

pathos emotion

patrician aristocrat

patrimony inheritance

patronize condescend

patronymic a name formed form the name of a father

patter walk lightly

paucity scarcity

Quiz 23 (Matching)

Match each word in the first column with its definition in the second column.
Answers are on page 101.

1.	ORDNANCE	A.	a model
2.	ORTHODOX	B.	local speech
3.	OUTMODED	C.	convulsion
4.	PALAVER	D.	stingy
5.	PANEGYRIC	E.	agent causing disease
6.	PARADIGM	F.	artillery
7.	PARLANCE	G.	conventional
8.	PAROXYSM	H.	out-of-date
9.	PARSIMONIOUS	I.	babble
10.	PATHOGEN	J.	praise

paunch stomach

pauper poor person

pavilion tent

pawn (noun) tool, stooge

pawn (verb) pledge

pax peace

peaked wan, pale, haggard

peal reverberation, outburst

peccadillo a minor fault

peculate embezzle

peculiar unusual

peculiarity characteristic

pedagogical pertaining to teaching

pedagogue dull, formal teacher

pedant pedagogue

pedantic bookish

peddle sell

pedestrian common

pedigree genealogy

peerage aristocracy

peevish cranky

pejorative insulting

pell-mell in a confused manner

pellucid transparent

pen write

penance atonement

penchant inclination

pend depend, hang

pending not decided, awaiting

penitent repentant

pensive sad

penurious stingy

penury poverty

peon common worker

per se in itself

perceptive discerning

percolate ooze, permeate

perdition damnation

peregrination wandering

peremptory dictatorial

perennial enduring, lasting

perfectionist purist, precisionist

perfidious treacherous (of a person)

perforate puncture

perforce by necessity

perfunctory careless

perigee point nearest to the earth

perilous dangerous

peripatetic walking about

periphery outer boundary

perish die

perishable decomposable

perjury lying

permeate spread throughout

permutation reordering

pernicious destructive, evil

peroration conclusion

perpendicular at right angles

perpetrate commit

perpetual continuous, everlasting

perpetuate cause to continue

perpetuity eternity

perplex puzzle, bewilder

perquisite reward, bonus

persecute harass

persevere persist, endure

persona social facade

personable charming, friendly

personage official, dignitary

personify embody, exemplify

personnel employees

perspicacious keen

perspicacity discernment, keenness

persuasive convincing

pert flippant, bold

pertain to relate

pertinacious persevering

pertinent relevant

perturbation agitation

peruse read carefully

pervade permeate

pessimist cynic, naysayer

pestilence disease

petite small

petition a written request

petrify calcify, shock

petrology study of rocks

pettifogger unscrupulous lawyer

petty trivial, niggling

petulant irritable, peevish

phantasm apparition

phenomena unusual natural events

philanthropic charitable

philanthropist altruist

philatelist stamp collector

philippic invective

Philistine barbarian

philosophical contemplative

Quiz 24 (Analogies)

Directions: Choose the pair that expresses a relationship most similar to that expressed in the capitalized pair. Answers are on page 101.

1. SECLUSION : HERMIT ::

   (A) wealth: embezzler
   (B) ambition : philanthropist
   (C) domination : athlete
   (D) turpitude : introvert
   (E) injustice : lawyer

2. ASCETIC : SELF-DENIAL ::

   (A) soldier : safety
   (B) official : charity
   (C) thug : acceptance
   (D) benefactor : competition
   (E) profligate : squandering

3. Philanthropist : Altruism ::

   (A) authoritarian : indulgence
   (B) polemicist : Marxist
   (C) benefactor : heir
   (D) pragmatist : hard-liner
   (E) libertarian : liberty

4. RACONTEUR : ANECDOTE ::

   (A) cynosure : interest
   (B) politician : corruption
   (C) athlete : perfection
   (D) writer : publication
   (E) nonentity : fame

5. PATENT : MANIFEST ::

   (A) credulous : gullible
   (B) truculent : nonchalant
   (C) lissome : spiritless
   (D) covert : prolific
   (E) cloyed : insufficient

6. CENSORIOUS : CONDONING ::

   (A) inattentive : neglectful
   (B) cursory : inept
   (C) defunct : exquisite
   (D) perfunctory : thorough
   (E) munificent : generous

7. PURGE : OPPONENT ::

   (A) entrench : comrade
   (B) elevate : criminal
   (C) liquidate : politician
   (D) desalinize : salt
   (E) assuage : reactionary

8. ISLAND : ATOLL ::

   (A) peninsula : archipelago
   (B) fire : spring
   (C) hand : glove
   (D) utensil : fork
   (E) smock : instrument

9. MNEMONIC : MEMORY ::

   (A) demonstration : manifestation
   (B) pacemaker : heartbeat
   (C) sanction : recall
   (D) rhetoric : treatise
   (E) impasse : fruition

10. EAT : GORGE ::

   (A) sprint : jog
   (B) snicker : smirk
   (C) read : write
   (D) disengage : attack
   (E) drink : guzzle

phlegmatic sluggish

phobia fear

phoenix rebirth

physic laxative, cathartic

physique frame, musculature

picaresque roguish, adventurous

picayune trifling

piecemeal one at a time

pied mottled, brindled

piety devoutness

pilfer steal

pillage plunder

pillory punish by ridicule

pine languish, to long for someone or something

pinnacle highest point

pious devout, holy

piquant tart-tasting, spicy

pique sting, arouse interest

piscine pertaining to fish

piteous sorrowful, pathetic

pithy concise

pitiable miserable, wretched

pittance alms, driblet

pittance trifle

pivotal crucial

pixilated eccentric, possessed

placard poster

placate appease

placid serene

plagiarize pirate, counterfeit

plaintive expressing sorrow

platitude trite remark

platonic nonsexual

plaudit acclaim

pleasantry banter, persiflage

plebeian common, vulgar

plebiscite referendum

plenary full

plentiful abundant

pleonasm redundancy, verbosity

plethora overabundance

pliable flexible

pliant supple, flexible

plight sad situation

plucky courageous

plumb measure

plummet sudden short fall

plutocrat wealthy person

plutonium radioactive material

poach steal

podgy fat

podium stand, rostrum

pogrom massacre, mass murder

poignant pungent, sharp, heartbreaking

polemic a controversy

polity methods of government

poltroon dastard

polychromatic many-colored

polygamist one who has many wives

ponder muse, reflect

ponderous heavy, bulky

pontiff bishop

pontificate to speak at length

pootroon coward

porcine pig-like

porous permeable, spongy

porridge stew

portend signify, augur

portent omen

portly large

portmanteau suitcase

posit stipulate

posterior rear, subsequent

posterity future generations

posthaste hastily

posthumous after death

postulate supposition, premise

potent powerful

potentate sovereign, king

potion brew

potpourri medley

potter aimlessly busy

pragmatic practical

prate babble

prattle chatter

preamble introduction

precarious dangerous, risky

precedent an act that serves as an example

precept principle, law

precinct neighborhood

precipice cliff

precipitate cause

precipitous steep

précis summary

precise accurate, detailed

preclude prevent

precocious more developed than is expected at a particular age

preconception prejudgment, prejudice

precursor forerunner

predacious plundering

predecessor one who proceeds

predestine foreordain

predicament quandary

predicate to base an opinion on something

predilection inclination

predisposed inclined

preeminent supreme

preempt commandeer

preen groom

prefabricated ready-built

prefect magistrate

preference choice

preferment promotion

prelate primate, bishop

preliminary introductory

prelude introduction

premeditate plan in advance

premonition warning

prenatal before birth

Quiz 25 (Matching)

Match each word in the first column with its definition in the second column.
Answers are on page 102.

1.	PHOENIX	A.	cliff
2.	PILLORY	B.	inclination
3.	PITTANCE	C.	warning
4.	PLAUDIT	D.	acclaim
5.	PLETHORA	E.	overabundance
6.	POGROM	F.	after death
7.	POSTHUMOUS	G.	massacre
8.	PRECIPICE	H.	rebirth
9.	PREDILECTION	I.	punish by ridicule
10.	PREMONITION	J.	trifle

preponderance predominance

prepossessing appealing, charming

preposterous ridiculous

prerequisite requirement

prerogative right, privilege

presage omen

prescribe urge

presentable acceptable, well-mannered

preside direct, chair

pressing urgent

prestidigitator magician

prestige reputation, renown

presume assume, deduce

presumptuous assuming, overconfident

presuppose assume

pretense affectation, excuse

pretentious affected, inflated

preternatural abnormal, supernatural

pretext excuse

prevail triumph

prevailing common, current

prevalent widespread

prevaricate lie

prick puncture

priggish pedantic, affected

prim formal, prudish

primal first, beginning

primate head, master

primogeniture first-born child

primp groom

princely regal, generous

prismatic many-colored, sparkling

pristine pure, unspoiled

privation hardship

privy aware of private matters

probe examine

probity integrity

problematic uncertain, difficult

proboscis snout

procedure method, process

proceeds profit

proclaim announce

proclivity inclination

procreate beget

proctor supervise

procure acquire

procurer pander

prod urge

prodigal wasteful

prodigious marvelous, enormous

prodigy a person with extraordinary ability or talent

profane blasphemous

profess affirm, admit

proffer bring forward for consideration

proficient skillful

profiteer extortionist

profligate licentious, prodigal

profound deep, knowledgeable

profusion overabundance

progenitor ancestor

progeny children

prognosis forecast

prognosticate foretell

progressive advancing, liberal

proletariat working class

proliferate increase rapidly

prolific fruitful, productive

prolix long-winded

prologue introduction

prolong lengthen in time

promenade stroll, parade

promethean inspirational

promiscuous sexually indiscreet

promontory headland, cape

prompt induce

prompter reminder

promulgate publish, disseminate

prone inclined, predisposed

propaganda publicity, misinformation

propellant rocket fuel

propensity inclination

prophet prognosticator

prophylactic preventive

propinquity nearness

propitiate satisfy

propitious auspicious, favorable

proponent supporter, advocate

proportionate commensurate

proposition offer, proposal

propound propose

proprietor manager, owner

propriety decorum

prosaic uninspired, flat

proscenium platform, rostrum

proscribe prohibit

proselytize recruit, convert

prosody study of poetic structure

Quiz 26 (Analogies)

<u>Directions:</u> Choose the pair that expresses a relationship most similar to that expressed in the capitalized pair. Answers are on page 102.

1. CALLOUS : SYMPATHY ::

    (A)   flawless : excellence
    (B)   histrionic : theatrics
    (C)   outgoing : inhibition
    (D)   indiscreet : platitude
    (E)   categorical : truism

2. INSIPID : TASTE ::

    (A)   curt : incivility
    (B)   apathetic : zest
    (C)   immaculate : brevity
    (D)   trite : unimportance
    (E)   discriminating : scholarship

3. Apocryphal : Corroboration ::

    (A)   didactic : instruction
    (B)   fraudulent : forgery
    (C)   tyrannical : poise
    (D)   esoteric : commonality
    (E)   sacrilegious : piety

4. NEBULOUS : DISTINCTION ::

    (A)   guileless : deceit
    (B)   antipathetic : abhorrence
    (C)   sublime : disrespect
    (D)   magnanimous : anxiety
    (E)   amorphous : inchoation

5. TARNISH : VITIATE ::

    (A)   beleaguer : console
    (B)   abrogate : flicker
    (C)   ensconce : corrupt
    (D)   bemuse : stupefy
    (E)   inundate : squelch

6. NOCTURNAL : CIMMERIAN ::

    (A)   exacting : lax
    (B)   prudish : indulgent
    (C)   contentious : affluent
    (D)   stark : embellished
    (E)   specious : illusory

7. CONVOCATION : MEETING ::

    (A)   bargain : market
    (B)   supplication : prayer
    (C)   issue : referendum
    (D)   speech : podium
    (E)   harvest : fall

8. OSTRICH : BIRD ::

    (A)   dusk : day
    (B)   fish : ocean
    (C)   tunnel : mountain
    (D)   hat : coat
    (E)   sirocco : storm

9. VIRUS : ORGANISM ::

    (A)   vegetable : mineral
    (B)   test-tube : bacteria
    (C)   microcosm : world
    (D)   microfiche : computer
    (E)   watch : wrist

10. Mercurial : Temperament ::

    (A)   capricious : interest
    (B)   tempestuous : solemnity
    (C)   staid : wantonness
    (D)   phlegmatic : concern
    (E)   cynical : naiveté

prospective expected, imminent

prospectus brochure

prostrate supine

protagonist main character in a story

protean changing readily

protégé ward, pupil

protocol code of diplomatic etiquette

proton particle

protract prolong

protuberance bulge

provender food

proverb maxim

proverbial well-known

providence foresight, divine protection

provident having foresight, thrifty

providential fortunate

province bailiwick, district

provincial intolerant, insular

provisional temporary

proviso stipulation

provisory conditional

provocation incitement

provocative titillating

provoke incite

prowess strength, expertise

proximity nearness

proxy substitute, agent

prude puritan

prudence discretion, carefulness

prudent cautious, using good judgment

prudish puritanical

prurient lewd

pseudo false

pseudonym alias

psychic pertaining the psyche or mind

psychopath madman

psychotic demented

puberty adolescence

puckish impish, mischievous

puerile childish

pugilism boxing

pugnacious combative

puissant strong

pulchritude beauty

pulp paste, mush

pulpit platform, priesthood

pulsate throb

pulverize crush

pun wordplay

punctilious meticulous

pundit learned or politically astute person

pungent sharp smell or taste

punitive punishing

puny weak, small

purblind obtuse, stupid

purgative cathartic, cleansing

purgatory limbo, netherworld

purge cleanse, remove

puritanical prim

purlieus environs, surroundings

purloin steal

purport claim to be

purported rumored

purposeful determined

pursuant following, according

purvey deliver, provide

purview range of understanding, field

pusillanimous cowardly

putative reputed

putrefy decay

putsch a sudden attempt to overthrow a government

pygmy dwarf

pyrotechnics fireworks

pyrrhic a battle won with unacceptable losses

Q

quack charlatan

quadrennial occurring every four years

quadrille square dance

quadruped four foot animal

quaff drink

quagmire difficult situation

quail shrink, cower

quaint old-fashioned, charming

qualified limited

qualms misgivings

quandary dilemma

quantum quantity, particle

quarantine detention, confinement

quarry prey, game

quarter residence, district

quash put down, suppress

quasi seeming, almost

quaver tremble

quay wharf

queasy squeamish

queer odd

quell suppress, allay

quench extinguish, slake

querulous complaining

questionnaire survey, feedback

queue line

quibble bicker

quicken revive, hasten

quiddity essence, an unimportant or trifling distinction

quiescent still, motionless

quietus a cessation of activity

quill feather, pen

quip joke

quirk eccentricity, a strange and unexpected turn of events

quiver tremble

quixotic impractical, romantic

quizzical odd, questioning

quorum the minimum number people who must be present to hold a meeting

quota a share or proportion

quotidian daily

Quiz 27 (Matching)

Match each word in the first column with its definition in the second column. Answers are on page 102.

1.	PROTEAN	A.	bulge
2.	PROTUBERANCE	B.	changing readily
3.	PROVISIONAL	C.	steal
4.	PUNDIT	D.	majority
5.	PURLOIN	E.	temporary
6.	PURPORT	F.	a cessation of activity
7.	QUAVER	G.	line
8.	QUEUE	H.	tremble
9.	QUIETUS	I.	claim to be
10.	QUORUM	J.	politically astute person

R

rabble crowd

rabid mad, furious

racketeer gangster, swindler

raconteur storyteller

radical revolutionary

raffish rowdy, dashing

rail rant, harangue

raiment clothing

rake womanizer

rally assemble

rambunctious boisterous

ramification consequence

rampage run amuck

rampant unbridled, raging

ramrod rod

rancid rotten

rancor resentment

randy vulgar

rankle cause bitterness, resentment

rant rage, scold

rapacious grasping, avaricious

rapidity speed

rapier sword

rapine plunder

rapport affinity, empathy

rapprochement reconciliation

rapture bliss

rash hasty, brash

rasp scrape

ratify approve

ration allowance, portion

rationale justification

ravage plunder, ruin

ravish captivate, charm

raze destroy or level a building

realm kingdom, domain

realpolitik cynical interpretation of politics

reap harvest

rebuff reject, snub

rebuke criticize, reprimand

rebus picture puzzle

rebuttal reply, counterargument

recalcitrant stubbornly resisting the authority of another

recant retract a previous statement

recapitulate restate, summarize

recede move back

receptacle container

receptive open to ideas

recidivism habitual criminal activity

recipient one who receives

reciprocal mutual, return in kind

recital performance, concert

recitation recital, lesson

reclusive solitary

recoil flinch, retreat

recollect remember

recompense repay, compensate

reconcile adjust, balance

recondite mystical, profound

reconnaissance surveillance

reconnoiter to survey, to scout (especially for military purposes)

recount recite

recoup recover

recourse appeal, resort

recreant cowardly

recrimination countercharge, retaliation

recruit draftee

rectify correct, to make right

recumbent reclining

recuperation recovery

recur repeat, revert

redeem buy back, justify, restore yourself to favor or to good opinion

redeemer savior

redemption salvation

redolent fragrant

redoubt fort

redoubtable formidable, steadfast

redress restitution, compensation

redundant repetitious

reek smell

reel stagger, to lurch backward as though struck by a blow

referendum vote

refined purified, cultured

reflux ebb

refraction bending, deflection

refractory obstinate, disobedient

refrain abstain

refurbish remodel, renovate

refute disprove, contradict

regal royal

regale entertain

regalia emblems

Quiz 28 (Analogies)

<u>Directions:</u> Choose the pair that expresses a relationship most similar to that expressed in the capitalized pair. Answers are on page 102.

1. PLUMMET : FALL ::

   (A) rifle : search
   (B) accelerate : stop
   (C) interdict : proscribe
   (D) rake : scour
   (E) precipitate : ascend

2. DRONE : EMOTION ::

   (A) sprint : journey
   (B) annoy : emollient
   (C) stupefy : erudition
   (D) deadpan : expression
   (E) scuttle : ship

3. MAROON : SEQUESTER ::

   (A) transfix : emote
   (B) exhaust : innervate
   (C) tranquilize : qualify
   (D) select : rebuff
   (E) entreat : beseech

4. TOTTER : WALK ::

   (A) annex : land
   (B) fathom : enlightenment
   (C) distend : contusion
   (D) efface : consolation
   (E) stutter : speech

5. LIGHT : DIM ::

   (A) indictment : investigate
   (B) protest : muffle
   (C) heat : radiate
   (D) solid : incinerate
   (E) ornament : decorate

6. BENIGN : PERNICIOUS ::

   (A) ostentatious : tawdry
   (B) mortified : nefarious
   (C) apocryphal : categorical
   (D) discerning : keen
   (E) pejorative : vicarious

7. Demagogue : Manipulator ::

   (A) champion : defender
   (B) lawyer : mediator
   (C) mentor : oppressor
   (D) soldier : landowner
   (E) capitalist : socialist

8. GREGARIOUS : CONGENIAL ::

   (A) suspicious : trusting
   (B) pedantic : lively
   (C) bellicose : militant
   (D) singular : nondescript
   (E) seminal : apocalyptic

9. DISHEARTENED : HOPE ::

   (A) enervated : ennui
   (B) buoyant : effervescence
   (C) amoral : ethics
   (D) munificent : altruism
   (E) nefarious : turpitude

10. PRATTLE : SPEAK ::

   (A) accept : reject
   (B) stomp : patter
   (C) heed : listen
   (D) promenade : walk
   (E) ejaculate : shout

regime a government

regiment infantry unit

regrettable lamentable, unfortunate

regurgitate vomit, repeat

rehash wearily discuss again

reign rule, influence

rein curb, restrain

reincarnation rebirth

reiterate repeat, say again

rejoice celebrate

rejoinder answer, retort

rejuvenate make young again

relapse recurrence (of illness)

relegate assign to an inferior position

relent soften, yield

relentless unstoppable

relic antique

relinquish release, renounce

relish savor

remedial corrective

remiss negligent

remit forgive, send payment

remnant residue, fragment

remonstrance protest

remorse guilt

remuneration compensation

renaissance rebirth

renascent reborn

rend to tear apart

render deliver, provide

rendezvous a meeting

rendition version, interpretation

renege break a promise

renounce disown

renown fame

rent tear, rupture

reparation amends, atonement

repartee witty conversation

repatriate to send back to the native land

repellent causing aversion

repent atone for

repercussion consequence

repertoire stock of works

repine fret

replenish refill

replete complete

replica copy

replicate duplicate

repose rest

reprehensible blameworthy

repress suppress

reprieve temporary suspension

reprimand rebuke

reprisal retaliation

reprise repetition

reproach blame

reprobate miscreant

reprove rebuke

repudiate disavow

repugnant distasteful, revolting

repulse repel

repulsive repugnant

repute status, reputation, esteem

reputed supposed, presumed, alleged

requiem rest, a mass for the dead

requisite necessary

requisition order, formal demand

requite to return in kind

rescind revoke

reserve self-control

reside dwell

residue remaining part

resigned accepting of a situation

resilience ability to recover from an illness or a setback

resolute determined

resolution determination

resolve determination

resonant reverberating

resort recourse

resound echo

resourceful inventive, skillful

respectively in that order

respire breathe

respite rest, temporary delay

resplendent shining, splendid

restitution reparation, amends

restive nervous, uneasy

resurgence revival

resurrection rebirth

resuscitate revive

retain keep

retainer advance fee

retaliate revenge

retch vomit

reticent reserved

retiring modest, unassuming

retort quick reply

retrench cut back, economize

retribution reprisal

retrieve reclaim

retrograde regress

retrospective reminiscent, display

revamp recast

reveille bugle call

revel frolic, take joy in

revelry merrymaking

revenue income

revere honor

reverent respectful

reverie daydream

revert return to a former state

revile denounce, defame

revision new version

revive renew

revoke repeal

revulsion aversion

rhapsody ecstasy

rhetoric elocution, grandiloquence

rheumatism inflammation

ribald coarse, vulgar

Quiz 29 (Matching)

Match each word in the first column with its definition in the second column.
Answers are on page 102.

1.	REGIME	A.	vulgar
2.	REJOINDER	B.	quick reply
3.	REMUNERATION	C.	uneasy
4.	RENDEZVOUS	D.	necessary
5.	RENT	E.	miscreant
6.	REPROBATE	F.	rupture
7.	REQUISITE	G.	a meeting
8.	RESTIVE	H.	compensation
9.	RETRIBUTION	I.	retort
10.	RIBALD	J.	a government

rickety shaky, ramshackle

ricochet carom, rebound

rife widespread, abundant

riffraff dregs of society

rifle search through and steal

rift a split, an opening, disagreement

righteous upright, moral

rigor harshness, precise and exacting

rime crust

riposte counterthrust

risible laughable

risqué off-color, racy

rivet engross

robust vigorous

rogue scoundrel

roister bluster

romp frolic

roseate rosy, optimistic

roster list of people

rostrum podium

roué libertine

rouse awaken, provoke

rout vanquish, cause to retreat

rubicund ruddy complexion

ruck the common herd

rudiment beginning, kernel

rue regret

ruffian brutal person

ruminate ponder

rummage hunt, grope

runel stream

ruse trick

rustic rural

S

Sabbath day of rest

sabbatical vacation

saber sword

sabotage treason, destruction

saccharine sugary, overly sweet tone

sacerdotal priestly

sack pillage

sacrament rite

sacred cow idol, taboo

sacrilege blasphemy

sacrosanct sacred

saddle encumber

sadist one who takes pleasure in hurting others

safari expedition

saga story

sagacious wise

sage wise person

salacious licentious

salient prominent

saline salty

sallow sickly complected

sally sortie, attack

salutary good, wholesome

salutation salute, greeting

salvation redemption

salve medicinal ointment

salvo volley, gunfire

sanctify consecrate

sanctimonious self-righteous

sanction approval

sanctuary refuge

sang-froid coolness under fire

sanguinary gory, murderous

sanguine cheerful

sans without

sapid interesting

sapient wise

sarcophagus stone coffin

scornful scornful, sarcastic

sartorial pertaining to clothes

satanic pertaining to the Devil

satchel bag

sate satisfy fully

satiate satisfy fully

satire ridicule

saturate soak

saturnine gloomy

satyr demigod, goat-man

saunter stroll

savanna grassland

savant scholar

savoir-faire tact, polish

savor enjoy, relish

savory appetizing

savvy perceptive, shrewd

scabrous difficult

scant inadequate, meager

scapegoat one who takes blame for others

scarify criticize

scathe injure, denounce

Quiz 30 (Analogies)

Directions: Choose the pair that expresses a relationship most similar to that expressed in the capitalized pair. Answers are on page 102.

1. THIMBLE : FINGER ::

   (A) glove : hammer
   (B) stitch : loop
   (C) branch : flower
   (D) talon : eagle
   (E) smock : apparel

2. ANARCHY : ORDER ::

   (A) desolation : annihilation
   (B) ineptitude : skill
   (C) bastion : aegis
   (D) chaos : disarray
   (E) parsimony : elegance

3. LAND : FALLOW ::

   (A) automobile : expensive
   (B) politics : innovative
   (C) orchard : fruitful
   (D) mountain : precipitous
   (E) ship : decommissioned

4. HEURISTIC : TEACH ::

   (A) parable : obfuscate
   (B) performer : entertain
   (C) pedant : construct
   (D) actor : incite
   (E) virus : prevent

5. RUSE : DECEIVE ::

   (A) pretext : mollify
   (B) invective : laud
   (C) cathartic : cleanse
   (D) artifice : disabuse
   (E) calumny : confuse

6. RETICENT : WANTON ::

   (A) lithe : supple
   (B) exemplary : palpable
   (C) pejorative : opprobrious
   (D) quiescent : rampant
   (E) provincial : virulent

7. GULLIBLE : DUPE ::

   (A) artless : demagogue
   (B) Machiavellian : entrepreneur
   (C) cantankerous : curmudgeon
   (D) disputatious : patron
   (E) optimistic : defeatist

8. OPAQUE : LIGHT ::

   (A) porous : liquid
   (B) undamped : vibration
   (C) unrelenting : barbarian
   (D) diaphanous : metal
   (E) hermetic : air

9. QUIXOTIC : PRAGMATIC ::

   (A) romantic : fanciful
   (B) dispassionate : just
   (C) auspicious : sanguine
   (D) malcontent : jingoistic
   (E) optimistic : surreal

10. COLON : INTRODUCE ::

    (A) hyphen : join
    (B) semicolon : transfer
    (C) dash : shorten
    (D) apostrophe : intensify
    (E) comma : possess

scepter a rod, staff

scheme plot, system, diagram

schism rift

scintilla speck

scintillate sparkle

scion offspring

scoff jeer, dismiss

scone biscuit

scorn disdain, reject

scoundrel unprincipled person

scour clean by rubbing, search

scourge affliction

scruples misgivings

scrupulous principled, fastidious

scrutinize examine closely

scurf dandruff

scurrilous abusive, insulting

scurry move quickly

scuttle to sink (a ship)

scythe long, curved blade

sear burn

sebaceous like fat

secede withdraw

secluded remote, isolated

seclusion solitude

sectarian denominational

secular worldly, nonreligious

secure make safe

sedation state of calm

sedentary stationary, inactive

sedition treason, inciting rebellion

seduce lure

sedulous diligent

seedy rundown, ramshackle

seemly proper, attractive

seethe fume, resent

seismic pertaining to earthquakes

seismology study of earthquakes

self-effacing modest

semantics study of word meanings

semblance likeness

seminal fundamental, decisive

semper fidelis always loyal

senescence old age

senescent aging

seniority privilege due to length of service

sensational outstanding, startling

sensible wise, prudent

sensory relating to the senses

sensualist epicure

sensuous appealing to the senses, enjoying luxury

sententious concise

sentient conscious

sentinel watchman

sepulcher tomb

sequacious dependent

sequel continuation, epilogue

sequester segregate

seraphic angelic

serendipity a knack for making fortunate discoveries

serene peaceful

serpentine winding and twisting

serried saw-toothed

serum vaccine

servile slavish

servitude forced labor

sessile permanently attached

session meeting

settee seat, sofa

sever cut in two

severance division

shallot onion

sham pretense, imposter

shambles disorder, mess

shard sharp fragment of glass

sheen luster

sheepish shy, embarrassed

shibboleth password

shirk evade (work)

sliver fragment, shaving

shoal reef

shoring supporting

shortcomings personal deficiencies

shrew virago

shrewd clever, cunning

shrill high-pitched

shun avoid, spurn

shunt turn aside

shyster unethical lawyer

sibilant a hissing sound

sibling brother or sister

sickle semicircular blade

sidereal pertaining to the stars

sidle move sideways, slither

siege blockade

sierra mountain range

sieve strainer

signatory signer

signet a seal

silhouette outline, profile

silo storage tower

simian monkey

simile figure of speech

simper smile, smirk

simulacrum vague likeness

sinecure position with little responsibility

sinewy fibrous, stringy

singe burn just the surface of something

singly one by one, individually

singular unique, extraordinary

sinister evil, malicious

sinistral left-handed

siphon extract, tap

sire forefather, to beget

siren temptress

site location

skeptical doubtful

skinflint miser

skirmish a small battle

Quiz 31 (Matching)

Match each word in the first column with its definition in the second column. Answers are on page 102.

1.	SCRUPLES	A.	figure of speech
2.	SCYTHE	B.	proper, attractive
3.	SEEMLY	C.	long, curved blade
4.	SENTENTIOUS	D.	left-handed
5.	SERENDIPITY	E.	pertaining to the stars
6.	SHIBBOLETH	F.	signer
7.	SIDEREAL	G.	making fortunate discoveries
8.	SIGNATORY	H.	password
9.	SIMILE	I.	misgivings
10.	SINISTRAL	J.	concise

skittish excitable, wary, jumpy

skulk sneak about

skullduggery trickery

slake quench

slander defame

slate list of candidate

slaver drivel, fawn

slay kill

sleight dexterity, skill

slew an abundance

slither slide, slink

slogan motto

sloth laziness

slovenly sloppy

smattering superficial knowledge

smelt refine metal

smirk smug look

smite strike, afflict

smock apron

snare trap

snide sarcastic, spiteful

snippet morsel, small piece

snivel whine, sniff

snub ignore, slight

snuff extinguish

sobriety composed, abstinent, sober

sobriquet nickname

socialite one who is prominent in society

sociology study of society

sodality companionship

sodden soaked

sojourn trip, stopover

solace consolation, comfort

solder fuse, weld

solecism ungrammatical construction

solemn serious, somber

solemnity seriousness

solicit request

solicitous considerate, concerned

soliloquy monologue

solstice furthest point

soluble dissolvable

solvent financially sound

somatic pertaining to the body

somber gloomy, solemn

somnambulist sleepwalker

somnolent sleepy

sonnet short poem

sonorous resonant, majestic

sop morsel, compensation, offering

sophistry specious reasoning

soporific sleep inducing

soprano high female voice

sordid foul, ignoble

sorority sisterhood

soubrette actress, ingenue

souse a drunk

sovereign monarch

spar fight

spasmodic intermittent, fitful

spate sudden outpouring

spawn produce

specimen sample

specious false but plausible reasoning

spectacle public display

spectral ghostly

spectrum range, gamut

speculate conjecture

speleologist one who studies caves

spew eject

spindle shaft

spindly tall and thin

spinster old maid

spire pinnacle

spirited lively

spirituous alcohol, intoxicating

spite malice, grudge

spittle spit

splay spread apart

spleen resentment, wrath

splenetic peevish

splurge indulge

spontaneous extemporaneous

sporadic occurring irregularly

sportive playful

spry nimble

spume foam, froth

spurious false, counterfeit

spurn to reject a person with scorn

squalid filthy

squall rain storm

squander waste

squelch crush, stifle

stagnant stale, motionless

staid demure, sedate

Quiz 32 (Analogies)

<u>Directions:</u> Choose the pair that expresses a relationship most similar to that expressed in the capitalized pair. Answers are on page 102.

1. PERSPICACIOUS : INSIGHT ::
   - (A) ardent : quickness
   - (B) warm : temperature
   - (C) wealthy : scarcity
   - (D) rapacious : magnanimity
   - (E) churlish : enmity

2. Unprecedented : Previous Occurrence ::
   - (A) naive : harmony
   - (B) incomparable : equal
   - (C) improper : vacillation
   - (D) eccentric : intensity
   - (E) random : recidivism

3. SNAKE : INVERTEBRATE ::
   - (A) dolphin : fish
   - (B) eagle : talon
   - (C) boa constrictor : backbone
   - (D) penguin : bird
   - (E) bat : insect

4. LIMERICK : POEM ::
   - (A) monologue : chorus
   - (B) sonnet : offering
   - (C) waltz : tango
   - (D) skull : skeleton
   - (E) aria : song

5. INTEREST : OBSESSION ::
   - (A) faith : caprice
   - (B) nonchalance : insouciance
   - (C) diligence : assiduity
   - (D) decimation : annihilation
   - (E) alacrity: procrastination

6. RESOLUTE : WILL ::
   - (A) violent : peacefulness
   - (B) fanatic : concern
   - (C) balky : contrary
   - (D) notorious : infamy
   - (E) virtuous : wholesomeness

7. ATOM : MATTER ::
   - (A) neutron : proton
   - (B) vegetable : animal
   - (C) molecule : element
   - (D) component : system
   - (E) pasture : herd

8. ACTORS : TROUPE ::
   - (A) plotters : cabal
   - (B) professors : tenure
   - (C) workers : bourgeoisie
   - (D) diplomats : government
   - (E) directors : cast

9. COFFER : VALUABLES ::
   - (A) mountain : avalanche
   - (B) book : paper
   - (C) vault : trifles
   - (D) sanctuary : refuge
   - (E) sea : waves

10. LION : CARNIVORE ::
   - (A) man : vegetarian
   - (B) ape : ponderer
   - (C) lizard : mammal
   - (D) buffalo : omnivore
   - (E) shark : scavenger

stalwart pillar, strong, loyal

stamina vigor, endurance

stanch loyal

stanchion prop, foundation

stanza division of a poem

stark desolate

startle surprise

stately impressive, noble

static inactive, immobile

statue regulation

staunch loyal

stave ward off

steadfast loyal

stealth secrecy, covertness

steeped soaked, infused

stenography shorthand

stentorian loud or declamatory in tone

sterling high quality

stern strict

stevedore longshoreman

stifle suppress

stigma mark of disgrace

stiletto dagger

stilted formal, stiff

stimulate excite

stint limit, assignment

stipend payment

stipulate specify, arrange

stodgy stuffy, pompous

stoic indifferent to pain or pleasure

stoke prod, fuel

stole long scarf

stolid impassive

stout stocky

strait distress

stratagem trick, military tactic

stratify form into layers

stratum layer

striate to mark with stripes

stricture censure, restriction

strife conflict

striking impressive, attractive

stringent severe, strict

strive endeavor

studious diligent

stultify inhibit, enfeeble

stunted arrested development

stupefy deaden, dumfound

stupendous astounding

stupor lethargy

stylize formalize, artificial artistic style

stymie hinder, thwart

suave smooth, charming

sub rosa in secret

subcutaneous beneath the skin

subdue conquer

subjugate suppress

sublet subcontract

sublimate to redirect forbidden impulses (usually sexual) into socially accepted activities

sublime lofty, excellent

sublunary earthly

submit yield, acquiesce

subordinate lower in rank

subsequent succeeding, following

subservient servile, submissive

subside diminish

subsidiary subordinate

subsidize financial assistance

substantiate verify

substantive substantial

subterfuge cunning, ruse

subterranean underground

subvert undermine

succor help, comfort

succulent juicy, delicious

succumb yield, submit

suffice adequate

suffrage vote

suffuse pervade, permeate

suggestive thought-provoking, risqué

sullen sulky, sour

sully stain

sultry sweltering

summon call for, arraign

sumptuous opulent, luscious

sunder split

sundry various

superb excellent

supercilious arrogant

supererogatory wanton, superfluous

superfluous overabundant

superimpose cover, place on top of

superintend supervise

superlative superior

supernumerary subordinate

supersede supplant

supervene ensue, follow

supervise oversee

supine lying on the back

supplant replace

supplication prayer

suppress subdue

surfeit overabundance

surly rude, crass

surmise to guess

surmount overcome

surname family name

surpass exceed, excel

surreal dreamlike

surreptitious secretive

surrogate substitute

surveillance close watch

susceptible vulnerable

suspend stop temporarily

sustenance food

susurrant whispering

suture surgical stitch

svelte slender

swank fashionable

swarthy dark (as in complexion)

Quiz 33 (Matching)

Match each word in the first column with its definition in the second column. Answers are on page 102.

1. STAVE
2. STEVEDORE
3. STRAIT
4. STUDIOUS
5. SUBJUGATE
6. SUBTERFUGE
7. SUNDRY
8. SUPERFLUOUS
9. SUPINE
10. SURREAL

A. distress
B. diligent
C. ward off
D. longshoreman
E. various
F. overabundant
G. suppress
H. cunning
I. dreamlike
J. lying on the back

swatch strip of fabric

sweltering hot

swivel a pivot

sybarite pleasure-seeker

sycophant flatterer, flunky

syllabicate divide into syllables

syllabus schedule

sylph a slim, graceful girl

sylvan rustic

symbiotic cooperative, working in close association

symmetry harmony, congruence

symposium panel (discussion)

symptomatic indicative

synagogue temple

syndicate cartel

syndrome set of symptoms

synod council

synopsis brief summary

synthesis combination

systole heart contraction

T

tabernacle temple

table postpone

tableau scene, backdrop

taboo prohibition

tabulate arrange

tacit understood without being spoken

taciturn untalkative

tactful sensitive

tactics strategy

tactile tangible

taint pollute

talion punishment

tally count

talon claw

tandem two or more things together

tang strong taste

tangential peripheral

tangible touchable

tantalize tease

tantamount equivalent

taper candle

tariff tax on imported or exported goods

tarn small lake

tarnish taint

tarry linger

taurine bull-like

taut tight

tautological repetitious

tawdry gaudy

technology body of knowledge

tedious boring, tiring

teem swarm, abound

temerity boldness

temperate moderate

tempest storm

tempestuous agitated

tempo speed

temporal pertaining to time

tempt entice

tenable defensible, valid

tenacious persistent

tendentious biased

tenement decaying apartment building

tenet doctrine

tensile stretchable

tentative provisional

tenuous thin, insubstantial

tenure status given after a period of time

tepid lukewarm

terminal final

terminology nomenclature

ternary triple

terpsichorean related to dance

terrain the feature of land

terrapin turtle

terrestrial earthly

terse concise

testament covenant

testy petulant

tether tie down

theatrics histrionics

theologian one who studies religion

thesaurus book of synonyms

thesis proposition, topic

thespian actor

thews muscles

thorny difficult

thrall slave

threadbare tattered

thrive prosper

throes anguish

throng crowd

throttle choke

thwart to foil

Quiz 34 (Matching)

Match each word in the first column with its definition in the second column.
Answers are on page 102.

1.	SWATCH	A.	to foil
2.	SYNOD	B.	anguish
3.	TACIT	C.	concise
4.	TALON	D.	provisional
5.	TAURINE	E.	agitated
6.	TEMPESTUOUS	F.	bull-like
7.	TENTATIVE	G.	claw
8.	TERSE	H.	understood without being spoken
9.	THROES	I.	council
10.	THWART	J.	strip of fabric

tiara crown

tidings news, information

tiff fight

timbre tonal quality, resonance

timorous fearful, timid

tincture trace, vestige, tint

tinsel tawdriness

tirade scolding speech

titan accomplished person

titanic huge

titer laugh nervously

tithe donate one-tenth

titian auburn

titillate arouse

titular in name only, figurehead

toady fawner, sycophant

tocsin alarm bell, signal

toil drudgery

tome large book

tonal pertaining to sound

topography science of map making

torment harass

torpid lethargic, inactive

torrid scorching, passionate

torsion twisting

torus doughnut shaped object

totter stagger

touchstone standard

tousled disheveled

tout praise, brag

toxicologist one who studies poisons

tractable docile, manageable

traduce slander

tranquilize calm, anesthetize

transcribe write a copy

transfigure transform, exalt

transfix impale

transfuse insert, infuse

transgression trespass, offense

transient fleeting, temporary

transitory fleeting

translucent clear, lucid

transpire happen

transpose interchange

trauma injury

travail work, drudgery

traverse cross

travesty caricature, farce

treatise book, dissertation

trek journey

trenchant incisive, penetrating

trepidation fear

triad group of three

tribunal court

tributary river

trite commonplace, insincere

troglodyte cave dweller

trollop harlot

troublous disturbed

trounce thrash

troupe group of actors

truckle yield

truculent fierce, savage

trudge march, slog

truism self-evident truth

truncate shorten

truncheon club

tryst meeting, rendezvous

tumbler drinking glass

tumefy swell

tumult commotion

turbid muddy, clouded

turgid swollen

turpitude depravity

tussle fight

tussock cluster of glass

tutelage guardianship

twain two

twinge pain

tyrannical dictatorial

tyranny oppression

tyro beginner

U

ubiquitous omnipresent, pervasive

ulterior hidden, covert

ultimatum demand

ululate howl, wail

umbrage resentment

unabashed shameless, brazen

unabated ceaseless

unaffected natural, sincere

unanimity agreement

unassuming modest

unavailing useless, futile

unawares suddenly, unexpectedly

unbecoming unfitting

unbridled unrestrained

Quiz 35 (Matching)

Match each word in the first column with its definition in the second column.
Answers are on page 102.

1.	TIDINGS	A.	incisive
2.	TITER	B.	omnipresent
3.	TITULAR	C.	lethargic
4.	TORPID	D.	figurehead
5.	TRADUCE	E.	unrestrained
6.	TRENCHANT	F.	news
7.	UBIQUITOUS	G.	laugh nervously
8.	ULULATE	H.	ceaseless
9.	UNABATED	I.	wail
10.	UNBRIDLED	J.	slander

uncanny mysterious, inexplicable

unconscionable unscrupulous

uncouth uncultured, crude

unctuous insincere

undermine weaken

underpin support

underscore emphasize

understudy a stand-in

underworld criminal world

underwrite agree to finance, guarantee

undue unjust, excessive

undulate surge, fluctuate

unduly excessive

unequivocal unambiguous, categorical

unexceptionable beyond criticism

unfailing steadfast, unfaltering

unfathomable puzzling, incomprehensible

unflagging untiring, unrelenting

unflappable not easily upset

unfrock discharge

unfurl open up, spread out

ungainly awkward

uniformity sameness

unilateral action taken by only one party

unimpeachable exemplary

unison together

unkempt disheveled

unmitigated complete, harsh

unmoved firm, steadfast

unprecedented without previous occurrence

unremitting relentless

unsavory distasteful, offensive

unscathed unhurt

unseat displace

unseemly unbecoming, improper

unstinting generous

unsullied spotless, pure

unsung neglected, not receiving just recognition

untenable cannot be achieved

untoward perverse, unseemly

unwarranted unjustified

unwieldy awkward

unwitting unintentional

upshot result

urbane refined, worldly

ursine bear-like

usurp seize, to appropriate

usury lending money at high rates

utilitarian pragmatic, useful

utopia paradise

utter complete

uxorious a doting husband

V

vacillate waver

vacuous inane, empty

vagary whim

vain unsuccessful

vainglorious conceited

valediction farewell speech

valiant brave

validate affirm, authenticate

valor bravery

vanguard leading position

vanquish conquer

vapid vacuous, insipid

variance discrepancy

vassal subject, subordinate

vaunt brag

vehement adamant

venal mercenary, for the sake of money

vendetta grudge, feud

veneer false front, facade

venerable revered

venial excusable

venom poison, spite

venture risk, speculate

venturesome bold, risky

venue location

veracity truthfulness

veranda porch

verbatim word for word, literal

verbose wordy

verdant green, lush

verdict decision, judgment

vernacular common speech

vertigo dizziness

vestige trace, remnant

veto reject

vex annoy

viable capable of surviving, feasible

viaduct waterway

Quiz 36 (Matching)

Match each word in the first column with its definition in the second column.
Answers are on page 102.

1.	UNCOUTH	A.	disheveled
2.	UNDULY	B.	capable of surviving
3.	UNFLAGGING	C.	awkward
4.	UNKEMPT	D.	uncultured
5.	UNSTINTING	E.	truthfulness
6.	UNTENABLE	F.	whim
7.	UNWIELDY	G.	unrelenting
8.	VAGARY	H.	cannot be achieved
9.	VERACITY	I.	generous
10.	VIABLE	J.	excessive

viand food

vicious evil, cruel

vicissitude changing fortunes

victuals food

vie compete

vigil watch, sentry duty

vigilant on guard

vignette scene

vigor vitality

vilify defame, malign

vindicate free from blame

vindictive revengeful

virile manly, strong

virtuoso highly skilled artist

virulent deadly, poisonous, infectious

visage facial expression

viscid thick, gummy

visitation a formal visit

vital necessary

vitiate spoil, ruin

vitreous glassy

vitriolic scathing

vituperative abusive, critical language

vivacious lively, high-spirited

vivid lifelike, clear

vivisection experimentation on animals, dissection

vocation occupation

vociferous adamant, clamoring

vogue fashion, chic

volant agile

volatile unstable, precarious

volition free will

voluble talkative

voluminous bulky, extensive

voracious hungry

votary fan, aficionado

vouchsafe confer, bestow

vulgarity obscenity

vulnerable susceptible

vulpine fox-like, cunning

W

wager bet

waggish playful

waive forego

wallow indulge

wan pale, pallid, listless

wane dissipate, wither

want need, poverty, lack of

wanton lewd, abandoned, gratuitous

warrant justification

wary guarded, cautious

wastrel spendthrift

waylay ambush, accost

wean remove from nursing, break a habit

weir dam

welter confusion, hodgepodge

wheedle to coax with flattery

whet stimulate

whiffle vacillate

whimsical capricious, playful

wield exercise control

willful deliberate, wanton

wily shrewd, crafty

wince cringe

windfall bonus, boon

winnow separate

winsome charmingly innocent

wistful sad yearning, melancholy

wither shrivel

wizened shriveled

woe anguish, despair

wont custom, habit

woo court, seek favor

wraith ghost

wrath anger, fury

wreak to inflict something violent

wrest snatch

wretched miserable

writ summons, court order

writhe contort, thrash about

wry twisted, ironic sense of humor

X

xenophillic attraction to strangers

xenophobia fear of foreigners

xylophone musical percussion instrument

Y

yarn story, tale

yearn desire strongly

yen desire, yearning

yore long ago

Young Turks reformers

Z

zeal earnestness, passion

zealot fanatic

zenith summit

zephyr gentle breeze

Quiz 37 (Sentence Completions)

Complete each sentence with the best available word. Answers are on page 102.

1. Though most explicitly sexist words have been replaced by gender-neutral terms, sexism thrives in the _____ of many words.

    (A)   indistinctness
    (B)   similitude
    (C)   loquacity
    (D)   implications
    (E)   obscurity

2. The aspiring candidate's performance in the debate all but _____ any hope he may have had of winning the election.

    (A)   nullifies
    (B)   encourages
    (C)   guarantees
    (D)   accentuates
    (E)   contains

3. She is the most _____ person I have ever met, seemingly with an endless reserve of energy.

    (A)   jejune
    (B)   vivacious
    (C)   solicitous
    (D)   impudent
    (E)   indolent

4. Despite all its _____, a stint in the diplomatic core is invariably an uplifting experience.

    (A)   merits
    (B)   compensation
    (C)   effectiveness
    (D)   rigors
    (E)   mediocrity

5. Robert Williams' style of writing has an air of _____: just when you think the story line is predictable, he suddenly takes a different direction. Although this is often the mark of a beginner, Williams pulls it off masterfully.

    (A)   ineptness
    (B)   indignation
    (C)   reserve
    (D)   jollity
    (E)   capriciousness

6. Though a small man, J. Edgar Hoover appeared to be much larger behind his desk; for, having skillfully designed his office, he was _____ by the perspective.

   (A) augmented
   (B) comforted
   (C) apprehended
   (D) lessened
   (E) disconcerted

7. Existentialism can be used to rationalize evil: if one does not like the rules of society and has no conscience, he may use existentialism as a means of _____ a set of beliefs that are advantageous to him but injurious to others.

   (A) thwarting
   (B) proving
   (C) promoting
   (D) justifying
   (E) impugning

8. These categories amply point out the fundamental desire that people have to express themselves and the cleverness they display in that expression; who would have believed that the drab, mundane DMV would become the _____ such creativity?

   (A) catalyst for
   (B) inhibitor of
   (C) disabler of
   (D) referee of
   (E) censor of

9. This argues well that Erikson exercised less free will than Warner; for even though Erikson was aware that he was misdirected, he was still unable to _____ free will.

   (A) defer
   (B) facilitate
   (C) proscribe
   (D) prevent
   (E) exert

10. Man has no choice but to seek truth, he is made uncomfortable and frustrated without truth—thus, the quest for truth is part of what makes us _____ .

   (A) noble
   (B) different
   (C) human
   (D) intelligent
   (E) aggressive

Answers to Quizzes

Quiz 1	Quiz 2	Quiz 3	Quiz 4	Quiz 5	Quiz 6	Quiz 7	Quiz 8
1. I	1. E	1. B	1. A	1. J	1. E	1. A	1. E
2. G	2. B	2. F	2. C	2. I	2. A	2. J	2. B
3. E	3. D	3. G	3. E	3. H	3. C	3. I	3. D
4. F	4. A	4. H	4. A	4. G	4. E	4. E	4. E
5. C	5. E	5. E	5. A	5. F	5. D	5. D	5. E
6. D	6. A	6. A	6. E	6. E	6. A	6. G	6 E
7. B	7. C	7. C	7. A	7. D	7. C	7. F	7. C
8. J	8. D	8. D	8. B	8. C	8. B	8. H	8. E
9. A	9. B	9. J	9. C	9. B	9. E	9. C	9. D
10. H	10. A	10. I	10. C	10. A	10. B	10. B	10. C

Quiz 9	Quiz 10	Quiz 11	Quiz 12	Quiz 13	Quiz 14	Quiz 15	Quiz 16
1. B	1. B	1. D	1. A	1. B	1. D	1. J	1. B
2. A	2. C	2. J	2. B	2. A	2. E	2. I	2. E
3. D	3. D	3. I	3. D	3. J	3. B	3. H	3. A
4. C	4. A	4. A	4. D	4. H	4. B	4. G	4. E
5. F	5. E	5. F	5. A	5. I	5. C	5. F	5. D
6. E	6. B	6. E	6. B	6. G	6. D	6. E	6. A
7. H	7. C	7. H	7. C	7. F	7. C	7. D	7. E
8. G	8. A	8. G	8. A	8. D	8. C	8. C	8. B
9. J	9. B	9. C	9. D	9. E	9. B	9. B	9. D
10. I	10. E	10. B	10. B	10. C	10. C	10. A	10. C

Quiz 17	Quiz 18	Quiz 19	Quiz 20	Quiz 21	Quiz 22	Quiz 23	Quiz 24
1. E	1. D	1. D	1. A	1. J	1. E	1. F	1. A
2. F	2. B	2. E	2. D	2. F	2. E	2. G	2. E
3. G	3. E	3. F	3. D	3. I	3. C	3. H	3. E
4. H	4. C	4. A	4. C	4. H	4. B	4. I	4. A
5. A	5. A	5. B	5. B	5. G	5. E	5. J	5. A
6. B	6. B	6. C	6. A	6. B	6. E	6. A	6. D
7. C	7. E	7. G	7. C	7. E	7. A	7. B	7. D
8. D	8. A	8. J	8. B	8. D	8. C	8. C	8. D
9. I	9. A	9. I	9. C	9. C	9. D	9. D	9. B
10. J	10. E	10. H	10. E	10. A	10. C	10. E	10. E

Quiz 25	Quiz 26	Quiz 27	Quiz 28	Quiz 29	Quiz 30	Quiz 31	Quiz 32
1. H	1. C	1. B	1. A	1. J	1. E	1. I	1. E
2. I	2. B	2. A	2. D	2. I	2. B	2. C	2. B
3. J	3. E	3. E	3. E	3. H	3. E	3. B	3. D
4. D	4. A	4. J	4. E	4. G	4. B	4. J	4. E
5. E	5. D	5. C	5. B	5. F	5. C	5. G	5. D
6. G	6. E	6. I	6. C	6. E	6. D	6. H	6. B
7. F	7. B	7. H	7. A	7. D	7. C	7. E	7. D
8. A	8. E	8. G	8. C	8. C	8. E	8. F	8. A
9. B	9. C	9. F	9. C	9. B	9. D	9. A	9. D
10. C	10. A	10. D	10. D	10. A	10. A	10. D	10. E

Quiz 33	Quiz 34	Quiz 35	Quiz 36	Quiz 37
1. C	1. J	1. F	1. D	1. D
2. D	2. I	2. G	2. J	2. A
3. A	3. H	3. D	3. G	3. B
4. B	4. G	4. C	4. A	4. D
5. G	5. F	5. J	5. I	5. E
6. H	6. E	6. A	6. H	6. A
7. E	7. D	7. B	7. C	7. D
8. F	8. C	8. I	8. F	8. A
9. J	9. B	9. H	9. E	9. E
10. I	10. A	10. E	10. B	10. C

Word Analysis

Word analysis (etymology) is the process of separating a word into its parts and then using the meanings of those parts to deduce the meaning of the original word. Take, for example, the word INTERMINABLE. It is made up of three parts: a prefix IN (not), a root TERMIN (stop), and a suffix ABLE (can do). Therefore, by word analysis, INTERMINABLE means "not able to stop." This is not the literal meaning of INTERMINABLE (endless), but it is close enough. For another example, consider the word RETROSPECT. It is made up of the prefix RETRO (back) and the root SPECT (to look). Hence, RETROSPECT means "to look back (in time), to contemplate."

Word analysis is very effective in decoding the meaning of words. However, you must be careful in its application since words do not always have the same meaning as the sum of the meanings of their parts. In fact, on occasion words can have the opposite meaning of their parts. For example, by word analysis the word AWFUL should mean "full of awe," or awe-inspiring. But over the years, it has come to mean just the opposite—terrible. In spite of the shortcomings, word analysis gives the correct meaning of a word (or at least a hint of it) far more often than not and therefore is a useful tool.

Examples:

INDEFATIGABLE

Analysis: IN (not);   DE (thoroughly);   FATIG (fatigue);   ABLE (can do)
Meaning: cannot be fatigued, tireless

CIRCUMSPECT

Analysis: CIRCUM (around);   SPECT (to look)
Meaning: to look around, that is, to be cautious

ANTIPATHY

Analysis: ANTI (against);   PATH (to feel);   Y (noun suffix)
Meaning: to feel strongly against something, to hate

OMNISCIENT

Analysis: OMNI (all);   SCI (to know);   ENT (noun suffix)
Meaning: all-knowing

Following are some of the most useful prefixes, roots, and suffixes.

Prefixes

1.	**ab**	from	aberration
2.	**ad**—also **ac, af, ag, al, an, ap, ar, as, at**	to	adequate
3.	**ambi**	both	ambidextrous
4.	**an**—also **a**	without	anarchy
5.	**anti**	against	antipathetic
6.	**ante**	before	antecedent
7.	**be**	throughout	belie
8.	**bi**	two	bilateral
9.	**cata**	down	catacomb
10.	**circum**	around	circumscribe
11.	**com**—also **con, col, cor, cog, co**	together	confluence
12.	**contra**	against	contravene
13.	**de**	down (negative)	debase
14.	**deca**	ten	decathlon
15.	**decem**	ten	decimal
16.	**di**	two	digraph
17.	**dia**	through, between	dialectic
18.	**dis**	apart (negative)	disparity
19.	**du**	two	duplicate
20.	**dys**	abnormal	dysphoria
21.	**epi**	upon	epicenter
22.	**equi**	equal	equitable
23.	**ex**	out	extricate
24.	**extra**	beyond	extraterrestrial
25.	**fore**	in front of	foreword
26.	**hemi**	half	hemisphere
27.	**hyper**	excessive	hyperbole
28.	**hypo**	too little	hypothermia
29.	**in**—also **ig, il, im, ir**	not	inefficient

30. **in**—also **il, im, ir**	in, very	invite, inflammable
31. **inter**	between	interloper
32. **intro**—also **intra**	inside	introspective
33. **kilo**	one thousand	kilogram
34. **meta**	changing	metaphysics
35. **micro**	small	microcosm
36. **mili**—also **milli**	one thousand	millipede
37. **mis**	bad, hate	misanthrope
38. **mono**	one	monopoly
39. **multi**	many	multifarious
40. **neo**	new	neophyte
41. **nil**—also **nihil**	nothing	nihilism
42. **non**	not	nonentity
43. **ob**—also **oc, of, op**	against	obstinate
44. **pan**	all	panegyric
45. **para**	beside	paranormal
46. **per**	throughout	permeate
47. **peri**	around	periscope
48. **poly**	many	polyglot
49. **post**	after	posterity
50. **pre**	before	predecessor
51. **prim**	first	primitive
52. **pro**	forward	procession
53. **quad**	four	quadruple
54. **re**	again	reiterate
55. **retro**	backward	retrograde
56. **semi**	half	semiliterate
57. **sub**—also **suc, suf, sug, sup, sus**	under	succumb
58. **super**—also **supra**	above	superannuated
59. **syn**—also **sym, syl**	together	synthesis
60. **trans**	across	transgression
61. **un**	not	unkempt

62. **uni**	one	unique

Roots

Root	Meaning	Example
1. **ac**	bitter, sharp	acrid
2. **agog**	leader	demagogue
3. **agri**—also **agrari**	field	agriculture
4. **ali**	other	alienate
5. **alt**	high	altostratus
6. **alter**	other	alternative
7. **am**	love	amiable
8. **anim**	soul	animadversion
9. **anthrop**	man, people	anthropology
10. **arch**	ruler	monarch
11. **aud**	hear	auditory
12. **auto**	self	autocracy
13. **belli**	war	bellicose
14. **ben**	good	benevolence
15. **biblio**	book	bibliophile
16. **bio**	life	biosphere
17. **cap**	take	caprice
18. **capit**	head	capitulate
19. **carn**	flesh	incarnate
20. **ced**	go	accede
21. **celer**	swift	accelerate
22. **cent**	one hundred	centurion
23. **chron**	time	chronology
24. **cide**	cut, kill	fratricide
25. **cit**	to call	recite
26. **civ**	citizen	civility
27. **cord**	heart	cordial
28. **corp**	body	corporeal

29.	**cosm**	universe	cosmopolitan
30.	**crat**	power	plutocrat
31.	**cred**	belief	incredulous
32.	**cur**	to care	curable
33.	**deb**	debt	debit
34.	**dem**	people	demagogue
35.	**dic**	to say	Dictaphone
36.	**doc**	to teach	doctorate
37.	**dynam**	power	dynamism
38.	**ego**	I	egocentric
39.	**err**	to wander	errant
40.	**eu**	good	euphemism
41.	**fac**—also **fic, fec, fect**	to make	affectation
42.	**fall**	false	infallible
43.	**fer**	to carry	fertile
44.	**fid**	faith	confidence
45.	**fin**	end	finish
46.	**fort**	strong	fortitude
47.	**gen**	race, group	genocide
48.	**geo**	earth	geology
49.	**germ**	vital part	germane
50.	**gest**	carry	gesticulate
51.	**gnosi**	know	prognosis
52.	**grad**—also **gress**	step	transgress
53.	**graph**	writing	calligraphy
54.	**grav**	heavy	gravitate
55.	**greg**	crowd	egregious
56.	**habit**	to have, live	habituate
57.	**hema**—also **hemo**	blood	hemorrhage
58.	**hetero**	different	heterogeneous
59.	**homo**	same	homogenized
60.	**hum**	earth, man	humble
61.	**jac**—also **jec**	throw	interjection

62. **jud**	judge	judicious
63. **junct**—also **join**	combine	disjunctive
64. **jus**—also **jur**	law, to swear	adjure
65. **leg**	law	legislator
66. **liber**	free	libertine
67. **lic**	permit	illicit
68. **loc**	place	locomotion
69. **log**	word	logic
70. **loqu**	speak	soliloquy
71. **macro**	large	macrobiotics
72. **magn**	large	magnanimous
73. **mal**	bad	malevolent
74. **manu**	by hand	manuscript
75. **matr**	mother	matriarch
76. **medi**	middle	medieval
77. **meter**	measure	perimeter
78. **mit**—also **miss**	send	missive
79. **morph**	form, structure	anthropomorphic
80. **mut**	change	immutable
81. **nat**—also **nasc**	born	nascent
82. **neg**	deny	renegade
83. **nomen**	name	nominal
84. **nov**	new	innovative
85. **omni**	all	omniscient
86. **oper**—also **opus**	work	operative
87. **pac**—also **plais**	please	complaisant
88. **pater**—also **patr**	father	expatriate
89. **path**	disease, feeling	pathos
90. **ped**—also **pod**	foot	pedestal
91. **pel**—also **puls**	push	impulsive
92. **pen**	hang	appendix
93. **phil**	love	philanthropic
94. **pict**	paint	depict

95. **poli**	city	metropolis
96. **port**	carry	deportment
97. **pos**—also **pon**	to place	posit
98. **pot**	power	potentate
99. **put**	think	computer
100. **rect**—also **reg**	straight	rectitude
101. **ridi**—also **risi**	laughter	derision
102. **rog**	beg	interrogate
103. **rupt**	break	interruption
104. **sanct**	holy	sanctimonious
105. **sangui**	blood	sanguinary
106. **sat**	enough	satiate
107. **sci**	know	conscience
108. **scrib**—also **script**	to write	circumscribe
109. **sequ**—also **secu**	follow	sequence
110. **simil**—also **simul**	resembling	simile
111. **solv**—also **solut**	loosen	absolve
112. **soph**	wisdom	unsophisticated
113. **spec**	look	circumspect
114. **spir**	breathe	aspire
115. **strict**—also **string**	bind	astringent
116. **stru**	build	construe
117. **tact**—also **tang, tig**	touch	intangible
118. **techni**	skill	technique
119. **tempor**	time	temporal
120. **ten**	hold	tenacious
121. **term**	end	interminable
122. **terr**	earth	extraterrestrial
123. **test**	to witness	testimony
124. **the**	god	theocracy
125. **therm**	heat	thermodynamics
126. **tom**	cut	epitome
127. **tort**—also **tors**	twist	distortion

128. **tract**	draw, pull	abstract
129. **trib**	bestow	attribute
130. **trud** —also **trus**	push	protrude
131. **tuit** —also **tut**	teach	intuitive
132. **ultima**	last	penultimate
133. **ultra**	beyond	ultraviolet
134. **urb**	city	urbane
135. **vac**	empty	vacuous
136. **val**	strength, valor	valediction
137. **ven**	come	adventure
138. **ver**	true	veracity
139. **verb**	word	verbose
140. **vest**	clothe	travesty
141. **vic**	change	vicissitude
142. **vit** —also **viv**	alive	vivacious
143. **voc**	voice	vociferous
144. **vol**	wish	volition

Suffixes determine the part of speech a word belongs to. They are not as useful for determining a word's meaning as are roots and prefixes. Nevertheless, there are a few that are helpful.

Suffixes

Suffix	Meaning	Example
1. **able** — also **ible**	capable of	legible
2. **acy**	state of	celibacy
3. **ant**	full of	luxuriant
4. **ate**	to make	consecrate
5. **er, or**	one who	censor
6. **fic**	making	traffic
7. **ism**	belief	monotheism
8. **ist**	one who	fascist
9. **ize**	to make	victimize
10. **oid**	like	steroid
11. **ology**	study of	biology
12. **ose**	full of	verbose
13. **ous**	full of	fatuous
14. **tude**	state of	rectitude
15. **ure**	state of, act	primogeniture

Exercise:

Analyze and define the following words.

Example: **RETROGRADE**
                Analysis: retro (backward);   grade (step)
                Meaning: to step backward, to regress

1.   **CIRCUMNAVIGATE**
        Analysis:
        Meaning:

2.   **MISANTHROPE**
        Analysis:
        Meaning:

3.   **ANARCHY**
        Analysis:
        Meaning:

4.   **AUTOBIOGRAPHY**
        Analysis:
        Meaning:

5.   **INCREDULOUS**
        Analysis:
        Meaning:

6.   **EGOCENTRIC**
        Analysis:
        Meaning:

7.   **INFALLIBLE**
        Analysis:
        Meaning:

8.   **AMORAL**
        Analysis:
        Meaning:

9.   **INFIDEL**
        Analysis:
        Meaning:

10.   **NONENTITY**
        Analysis:
        Meaning:

11.   **CORPULENT**
        Analysis:
        Meaning:

12.   **IRREPARABLE**
        Analysis:
        Meaning:

13.   **INTROSPECTIVE**
        Analysis:
        Meaning:
14.   **IMMORTALITY**
        Analysis:
        Meaning:
15.   **BENEFACTOR**
        Analysis:
        Meaning:
16.   **DEGRADATION**
        Analysis:
        Meaning:
17.   **DISPASSIONATE**
        Analysis:
        Meaning:
18.   **APATHETIC**
        Analysis:
        Meaning:

Solutions to Exercise

1.   **CIRCUMNAVIGATE**

Analysis: CIRCUM (around);   NAV (to sail);   ATE (verb suffix)
Meaning: To sail around the world.

2.   **MISANTHROPE**

Analysis: MIS (bad, hate);   ANTHROP (man)
Meaning: One who hates all mankind.

3.   **ANARCHY**

Analysis: AN (without);   ARCH (ruler);   Y (noun suffix)
Meaning: Without rule, chaos.

4.   **AUTOBIOGRAPHY**

Analysis: AUTO (self);   BIO (life);   GRAPH (to write);   Y (noun suffix)
Meaning: One's written life story.

5.   **INCREDULOUS**

Analysis: IN (not);   CRED (belief);   OUS (adjective suffix)
Meaning: Doubtful, unbelieving.

6.   **EGOCENTRIC**

Analysis: EGO (self);   CENTR (center);   IC (adjective suffix)
Meaning: Self-centered.

7.   **INFALLIBLE**

Analysis: IN (not);   FALL (false);   IBLE (adjective suffix)
Meaning: Certain, cannot fail.

8.   **AMORAL**

Analysis: A (without);   MORAL (ethical)
Meaning: Without morals.

Note: AMORAL does not mean immoral; rather it means neither right nor wrong. Consider the following example: Little Susie, who does not realize that it is wrong to hit other people, hits little Bobby. She has committed an AMORAL act. However, if her mother explains to Susie that it is wrong to hit other people and she understands it but still hits Bobby, then she has committed an *immoral* act.

9.   **INFIDEL**

Analysis: IN (not);   FID (belief)
Meaning: One who does not believe (of religion).

10.   **NONENTITY**

Analysis: NON (not);   ENTITY (thing)
Meaning: A person of no significance.

11.   **CORPULENT**

Analysis: CORP (body);   LENT (adjective suffix)
Meaning: Obese.

12.   **IRREPARABLE**

Analysis: IR (not);   REPAR (to repair);   ABLE (can do)
Meaning: Something that cannot be repaired; a wrong so egregious it cannot be righted.

13.   **INTROSPECTIVE**

Analysis: INTRO (within);   SPECT (to look);   IVE (adjective suffix)
Meaning: To look inward, to analyze oneself.

14.   **IMMORTALITY**

Analysis: IM (not);   MORTAL (subject to death);   ITY (noun ending)
Meaning: Cannot die, will live forever.

15.   **BENEFACTOR**

Analysis: BENE (good);   FACT (to do);   OR (noun suffix [one who])
Meaning: One who does a good deed, a patron.

16. ## DEGRADATION

Analysis: DE (down—negative); GRADE (step); TION (noun suffix)
Meaning: The act of lowering someone socially or humiliating them.

17. ## DISPASSIONATE

Analysis: DIS (away—negative); PASS (to feel)
Meaning: Devoid of personal feeling, impartial.

18. ## APATHETIC

Analysis: A (without); PATH (to feel); IC (adjective ending)
Meaning: Without feeling; to be uninterested. (The apathetic voters.)

Vocabulary Drills

Many students write off questions that contain words they don't recognize. This is a mistake. This chapter will introduce numerous techniques that will decode unfamiliar words and prod your memory of words you only half-remember. With these techniques, you will often be able to squeeze out enough meaning from an unfamiliar word to answer a question correctly.

TECHNIQUES FOR LEARNING NEW VOCABULARY

Put The Definition In Your Own Words

The first technique for learning new words is to put the definition in your own words. It is best to try to condense the definition to only one or two words; this will make it easier to remember. You will find simple one or two word definitions provided for you in the list of 4000 essential words in this book. You may be even more likely to remember these, however, if you put the definitions in your own words. For example, take the word

Heinous

The definition of *heinous* is "abominable, vile." However, you may find it much easier to remember by the word

Horrible

Often the dictionary definition of a word can be simplified by condensing the definition into one word. Take, for example, the word

Expiate

The dictionary definition is "to put an end to; to extinguish guilt, to make amends for." This definition may be summed up by one word

Atone

Putting definitions in your own words makes them more familiar and therefore easier to remember.

Create A Word Picture

Creating mental word pictures is another visual technique that you can apply to many words. You may remember in grade school learning the difference between the word *principal* and the word *principle*. Your teacher probably told you that *principal* refers to "the leader of an educational institution" and the word ends with "pal." Your school principal wants to be your "pal," so this is easy to remember (after all, you always wanted to be best friends with your principal, right?). Your teacher gave you a mental word picture.

Let's take another word: *sovereign*. *Sovereign* means "monarch." The word itself contains the word *reign*. What do you think of when you think of *reign*? You probably think of a king—or a monarch. So, picture a king when you are trying to recall the meaning of *sovereign*, and it should be easy to remember.

How about *pestilence*. *Pestilence* means "disease." The word *pest* is in the word. Pests are common in a garden, and, unfortunately, they often cause diseases among the plants in a garden. So when you see this word, picture a garden and then picture all of the pests that bring diseases to your garden. Then you will remember the meaning of *pestilence*.

WHEN YOU DON'T KNOW THE WORD

As we mentioned, you can't possibly memorize the whole dictionary, and, while you can learn the words in a list of words that occur most frequently on the SAT, there will inevitably still be some that you do not know. Don't be discouraged. Again, there are some very effective techniques that can be applied when a word does not look familiar to you.

Put The Word In Context

In our daily speech, we combine words into phrases and sentences; rarely do we use a word by itself. This can cause words that we have little trouble understanding in sentences to suddenly appear unfamiliar when we view them in isolation. For example, take the word

Whet

Most people don't recognize it in isolation. Yet, most people understand it in the following phrase:

To whet your appetite

Whet means to "stimulate."

If you don't recognize the meaning of a word, think of a phrase in which you have heard it used.

For another example, take the word

Hallow

In isolation, it may seem unfamiliar to you. However, you probably understand its use in the phrase

The hallowed halls of academia

Hallow means "to make sacred, to honor."

Problem Set A:

For the following antonyms think of a common phrase in which the capitalized word is used.

Directions: For the following problems, choose the word most opposite in meaning to the capitalized word.

1. GRATUITOUS: (A) voluntary   (B) arduous   (C) solicitous
(D) righteous   (E) befitting

2. FALLOW: (A) fatuous   (B) productive   (C) bountiful
(D) pertinacious   (E) opprobrious

3. METTLE: (A) ad hoc   (B) perdition   (C) woe
(D) trepidation   (E) apathy

4. SAVANT: (A) dolt   (B) sage   (C) attaché
(D) apropos comment   (E) state of confusion

5. RIFE: (A) multitudinous   (B) blemished   (C) sturdy
(D) counterfeit   (E) sparse

6. ABRIDGE: (A) distend   (B) assail   (C) unfetter
(D) enfeeble   (E) prove

7. PRODIGAL: (A) bountiful   (B) dependent   (C) provident
(D) superfluous   (E) profligate

8. REQUIEM: (A) humility   (B) prerequisite   (C) resolution
(D) reign   (E) hiatus

9. METE: (A) indict   (B) convoke   (C) hamper
(D) disseminate   (E) deviate

10. SEVERANCE: (A) continuation   (B) dichotomy   (C) astringency
(D) disclosure   (E) remonstrance

Change The Word Into A More Common Form

Most words are built from other words. Although you may not know a given word, you may spot the root word from which it is derived and thereby deduce the meaning of the original word.

Example 1:   PERTURBATION: (A) impotence   (B) obstruction
(C) prediction   (D) equanimity   (E) chivalry

You may not know how to pronounce PERTURBATION let alone know what it means. However, changing its ending yields the more common form of the word "perturbed," which means "upset, agitated." The opposite of upset is calm, which is exactly what EQUANIMITY means. The answer is (D).

Example 2:   TEMPESTUOUS: (A) prodigal   (B) reticent
                   (C) serene   (D) phenomenal   (E) accountable

TEMPESTUOUS is a hard word. However, if we drop the ending "stuous" and add the letter "r" we get the common word "temper." The opposite of having a temper is being calm or SERENE. The answer is (C).

Problem Set B:

For each of the following problems change the capitalized word into a more common form of the word and then find its antonym.

1. HYPOCRITICAL: (A) forthright (B) judicious (C) circumspect
                  (D) puritanical (E) unorthodox

2. VOLUMINOUS: (A) obscure (B) cantankerous (C) unsubstantial
                (D) tenacious (E) opprobrious

3. FANATICISM: (A) delusion (B) fascism (C) remorse
                (D) cynicism (E) indifference

4. INTERMINABLE: (A) finite (B) jejune (C) tranquil
                  (D) incessant (E) imprudent

5. ORNATE: (A) Spartan (B) blemished (C) sturdy
            (D) counterfeit (E) temporary

6. MUTABILITY: (A) simplicity (B) apprehension (C) frailty
                (D) maverick (E) tenacity

7. VIRULENT: (A) benign (B) intrepid (C) malignant
              (D) hyperbolic (E) tentative

8. ABSTEMIOUS: (A) timely (B) immoderate (C) bellicose
                (D) servile (E) irreligious

9. VERBOSE: (A) subliminal (B) myopic (C) pithy
             (D) dauntless (E) ubiquitous

10. VISCID: (A) subtle (B) faint (C) slick (D) vicious
            (E) difficult

Test Words For Positive And Negative Connotations

Testing words for positive and negative connotations is a very effective technique. Surprisingly, you can often solve a problem knowing only that a given word has a negative connotation.

Example 1: REPUDIATE: (A) denounce   (B) deceive   (C) embrace   (D) fib   (E) generalize

You may not know what REPUDIATE means, but you probably sense that it has a negative connotation. Since we are looking for a word whose meaning is opposite of REPUDIATE, we eliminate any answer-choices that are also negative. Now, "denounce," "deceive," and "fib" are all, to varying degrees, negative. So, eliminate them. "Generalize" has a neutral connotation: it can be positive, negative, or neither. So, eliminate it as well. Hence, by process of elimination, the answer is (C), EMBRACE.

Example 2: NOXIOUS: (A) diffuse   (B) latent   (C) beneficial   (D) unique   (E) unjust

NOXIOUS has a negative connotation (strongly so). Therefore, we are looking for a word with a positive connotation. Now "diffuse" means "spread out, widely scattered." Hence, it is neutral in meaning, neither positive nor negative. Thus, we eliminate it. "Latent" and "unique" are also neutral in meaning, eliminate. "Unjust" has a negative connotation, eliminate. The only word remaining, BENEFICIAL, has a strongly positive connotation and is the answer.

➤ **Any SAT Word That Starts With "De," "Dis," or "Anti" Will Almost Certainly Be Negative.**

Examples: Degradation, Discrepancy, Discriminating, Debase, Antipathy

➤ **Any SAT Word That Includes The Notion of Going up Will Almost Certainly Be Positive, and any SAT Word That Includes The Notion of Going Down Will Almost Certainly Be Negative.**

Examples (positive): Elevate, Ascendancy, Lofty

Examples (negative): Decline, Subjugate, Suborn (to encourage false witness)

Problem Set C:

Solve the following problems by checking for positive and negative connotations.

1. DERISION: (A) urgency   (B) admonishment   (C) uniqueness
   (D) diversity   (E) acclaim

2. ANTIPATHY: (A) fondness   (B) disagreement   (C) boorishness
   (D) provocation   (E) opprobrium

3. CAJOLE: (A) implore   (B) glance at   (C) belittle   (D) ennoble
   (E) engender

4. CENSURE: (A) prevaricate   (B) titillate   (C) aggrandize
   (D) obscure   (E) sanction

5. ADULATION: (A) immutability   (B) reluctance   (C) reflection
   (D) defamation   (E) indifference

6. NOISOME: (A) salubrious   (B) affable   (C) multifarious
   (D) provident   (E) officious

7. CONSECRATE: (A) curb   (B) destroy   (C) curse   (D) inveigh
   (E) exculpate

8. ILLUSTRIOUS: (A) bellicose   (B) ignoble   (C) theoretical
   (D) esoteric   (E) immaculate

9. DEIGN: (A) inveigh   (B) gainsay   (C) speculate   (D) reject
   (E) laud

10. SUBTERFUGE: (A) bewilderment   (B) artlessness   (C) deceit
    (D) felicitation   (E) jeopardy

Be Alert To Secondary (Often Rare) Meanings Of Words

The SAT writers often use common words but with their uncommon meanings.

Example 1: CHAMPION: (A) relinquish   (B) contest   (C) oppress
(D) modify   (E) withhold

The common meaning of CHAMPION is "winner." Its opposite would be "loser." But no answer-choice given above is synonymous with "loser." CHAMPION also means to support or fight for someone else. (Think of the phrase "to champion a cause.") Hence, the answer is (C), OPPRESS.

Example 2: AIR: (A) release   (B) differ   (C) expose   (D) betray
(E) enshroud

AIR is commonly used as a noun—indicating that which we breathe. A secondary meaning for AIR is to discuss publicly. The opposite is to ENSHROUD, to hide, to conceal. Hence, the answer is (E).

Problem Set D:

In solving the following problems, look for secondary meanings.

1. CURB: (A) bridle   (B) encourage   (C) reproach   (D) ameliorate
(E) perjure

2. DOCUMENT: (A) copy   (B) implement   (C) gainsay   (D) blanch
(E) rant

3. FLUID: (A) radiant   (B) smooth   (C) solid   (D) balky
(E) craggy

4. BOLT: (A) linger   (B) refrain from   (C) subdue   (D) strip
(E) transgress

5. TABLE: (A) palliate   (B) acclimate   (C) garner   (D) propound
(E) expedite

6. HARBOR: (A) provide shelter   (B) banish   (C) acquiesce
(D) extol   (E) capitulate

7. FLOWER: (A) burgeon   (B) exact   (C) blight   (D) refute
(E) stabilize

8. STEEP: (A) desiccate   (B) intensify   (C) pontificate   (D) whet
(E) hamper

9. RENT: (A) reserved   (B) restored   (C) razed   (D) busy
    (E) kinetic

10. EXACT: (A) extract   (B) starve   (C) lecture   (D) menace
    (E) condone

Use Your Past Knowledge / Education

Since you are studying for the SAT, you have probably completed, or almost completed, your high school studies. Therefore, you have a wealth of knowledge from which to draw when it comes to examining the words that will appear on the test. In your classes, you studied history and probably one or more foreign languages. You may have even taken a Latin class. Because the English language has "borrowed" many words from other languages, especially Latin and French, these classes give you valuable clues to the meanings of many of the words you may come across.

Example 1:   NARCISSISTIC: (A) egocentric   (B) complacent
(C) pretentious   (D) unostentatious   (E) unassertive

You may remember Narcissus from one of your literature and Greek mythology classes. One version of the story of Narcissus relates a man who falls in love with his own reflection in a pool. Because of his requited love, he dies. As a man in love with his own reflection, he portrays self-love to the ultimate degree. A man like this is pretentious. *Unostentatious* is the opposite of *pretentious*. Hence, the answer is (D), UNOSTENTATIOUS.

Example 2: VERDANT: (A) naïve   (B) seasoned   (C) ignorant   (D) amateur   (E) innocent

Recall from your Spanish class that *verde* means "green" and from your French class that *vert* means "green" as well. These words may remind you of the word *verdant*, which also means "green" and can refer to being "green" in experience or judgment. Therefore, in this example, (B), SEASONED, is the answer because it means "experienced."

Problem Set E:

Use your past knowledge and education to solve the following problems.

1. BLARNEY: (A) eloquence   (B) loquacity   (C) volubleness
    (D)   taciturnity   (E) efficacy

2. BRAVADO: (A) valor   (B) brevity   (C) audacity   (D) cowardice
    (E) chauvinism

3. BLASÉ: (A) satiated   (B) humdrum   (C) provoked   (D) jovial
    (E) robust

4. SABOTAGE: (A) subvert   (B) advocate   (C) extricate
   (D) undermine   (E) emancipate

5. GRATIS: (A) unsatisfactory   (B) gratuitous   (C) baneful
   (D) commensurable   (E) extravagant

6. PROTÉGÉ: (A) prodigy   (B) pedagogue   (C) liegeman
   (D) prodigal   (E) imbecile

7. PEJORATIVE: (A) depreciatory   (B) candid   (C) ameliorative
   (D) disparaging   (E) veracious

8. AMOROUS: (A) abhorrent   (B) congenial   (C) unadorned
   (D) magnanimous   (E) menacing

9. ACQUIESCE: (A) concede   (B) bestow   (C) accede   (D) mete
   (E) dissent

10. INCOGNITO: (A) recondite   (B) palpable   (C) inconspicuous
    (D) occultation   (E) disguise

Points to Remember

Techniques To Learn New Words

- Put the definition in your own words
- Write down the words
- Use flashcards
- Create a word picture
- Set goals

When You Don't Know The Word

- Put the word in context
- Change the word into a more common form
- Test words for positive and negative connotation
- Watch out for eye-catchers
- Be alert to secondary (often rare) meanings of words
- Use your past education/knowledge

Tips

- If the word starts with "De," "Dis," or "Anti," the word most likely has a negative connotation.
- If the word contains the notion of going up, it will most likely have a positive connotation.
- If the word contains the notion of going down, it will most likely have a negative connotation.

Answers and Solutions to Problems

Set A	Set B	Set C	Set D	Set E
1. E	1. A	1. E	1. B	1. D
2. B	2. C	2. A	2. C	2. A
3. D	3. E	3. C	3. D	3. C
4. A	4. A	4. E	4. A	4. B
5. E	5. A	5. D	5. E	5. E
6. A	6. E	6. A	6. B	6. B
7. C	7. A	7. C	7. C	7. C
8. D	8. B	8. B	8. A	8. A
9. B	9. C	9. E	9. B	9. E
10. A	10. C	10. B	10. E	10. B

Problem Set A:

1. You may not recognize GRATUITOUS in isolation, but you probably understand it in the phrase: "Gratuitous sex and violence." GRATUITOUS means "freely given, uncalled for." The opposite is BEFITTING. The answer is (E).

2. Think of the phrase: "Fallow youth." FALLOW means idle. The opposite is PRODUCTIVE. The answer is (B).

3. Think of the phrase: "To test your mettle." (The large waves tested the surfer's mettle.) METTLE means "character, courage." The opposite is TREPIDATION, which means fear. The answer is (D).

4. Think of the description: "Idiot-savant." An idiot-savant is a person who exhibits the characteristics of both a mentally retarded person and a mental gifted person. SAVANT means "reflective thinker." The opposite is a DOLT. The answer is (A).

5. You may have heard RIFE used in the following manner: "The city is rife with crime." RIFE means "widespread, permeated." The opposite is SPARSE. The answer is (E).

6. Think of the description: "Unabridged dictionary." An unabridged dictionary is the unabbreviated version of a dictionary. Hence, ABRIDGE means "to shorten." The opposite is DISTEND: to swell or protrude. The answer is (A).

7. Think of the description: "Prodigal son." The prodigal son is the wasteful, spoiled son—a playboy. Hence, PRODIGAL means "immoderate." The opposite is PROVIDENT—frugal, careful. The answer is (C).

8. Think of the phrase: "Requiem for a heavyweight." REQUIEM means "a rest from an arduous task." The opposite is REIGN, the time spent in power or at the top. The answer is (D).

9. Think of the phrase: "to mete out justice." METE means "to dispense, to distribute." The opposite is to gather, which is the meaning of CONVOKE. The answer is (B).

10. Think of the description: "severance pay," which is the income you continue to receive after you have stopped working for a company. SEVERANCE means "the act of breaking off (or severing) a relationship." The opposite is to continue the relationship. The answer is (A).

Problem Set B:

1. HYPOCRITICAL contains the base word HYPOCRITE, one who deceives. The opposite is one who is honest and candid. The answer is (A), FORTHRIGHT.

2. Embedded in the word VOLUMINOUS is the word VOLUME. So, we are looking for a word that is related to size. The only answer-choice related to size is UNSUBSTANTIAL. The answer is (C). (VOLUMINOUS means "large.")

3. FANATICISM contains FANATIC, which in turn contains FAN. Now, at a sporting event, fans often become overenthusiastic, which is precisely the meaning of FANATIC. Thus, we are looking for a word that means unenthusiastic. That is the meaning of INDIFFERENCE. The answer is (E).

4. INTERMINABLE comes from the base word TERMINATE—to stop. Now, the prefix *in* means "not," so INTERMINABLE means "not able to stop." The only word that contains the notion of stopping or limitedness is FINITE. Hence, the answer is (A).

5. Changing the ending of ORNATE to "ment" yields the more familiar word ORNAMENT—a decoration. The opposite is undecorated. Now, the best answer-choice is SPARTAN, which means "plain or austere." The answer is (A).

6. Changing the ending of MUTABILITY from "ability" to "ate" yields the more common word MUTATE—to change. So, we're looking for a word that means "unchanging." TENACITY means "steadfastness in one's opinions." In other words, not changing one's opinion easily. The answer is (E).

7. Dropping "lent" from VIRULENT and adding "s" yields the common word VIRUS. A VIRUS is harmful, so we want a word that means harmless, which is precisely the meaning of BENIGN. The answer is (A).

8. ABSTEMIOUS comes from ABSTAIN—to refrain from doing. The opposite is to do too much. Now, IMMODERATE means "excessive, indulgent." Hence, the answer is (B).

9. VERBOSE contains the word VERB, which means "word." VERBOSE means "too many words, wordy." Now, PITHY means "well put, concise." Hence, the answer is (C).

10. You have probably never seen the word VISCID, but changing the ending yields viscous or viscosity. The viscosity of oil is a measure of the thickness or gumminess of oil. Hence, VISCID means thick or gummy, and the opposite of gummy is SLICK. The answer is (C).

Problem Set C:

1. Since DERISION starts with DE, it should be negative. So, we are looking for a positive word. "Urgency" and "admonishment" are both somewhat negative—eliminate. "Uniqueness" and "diversity" are both neutral—eliminate. Hence, by process of elimination, the answer is (E), "acclaim." DERISION means "scorn."

2. Since ANTIPATHY starts with ANTI, it is negative. "Disagreement" "boorishness," "provocation," and "opprobrium" are all negative to varying degrees. Hence, the answer is (A), "fondness." ANTIPATHY means "hatred."

3. CAJOLE has a positive connotation. "Implore," "ennoble," and "engender" are all neutral to positive, and they are all similar to CAJOLE—eliminate. "Glance at" is neutral—eliminate. Thus, by process of elimination, the answer is (C), "belittle." CAJOLE means "to encourage."

4. CENSURE is a hard word. Nonetheless, you may sense that it has a negative connotation. (It comes from the same root as does "censor.") Hence, we want a positive word. "Sanction" is the only positive word offered, and it is the answer. CENSURE means "to deplore." The answer is (E).

5. ADULATION has a positive connotation. "Immutability," "reluctance," "reflection," and "indifference" are all neutral in connotation—eliminate. Thus, by process of elimination, the answer is (D), "defamation." ADULATION means "praise, applause."

6. NOISOME is a very negative word, so we are looking for a very positive
    word. Now, "multifarious" is neutral: it means "diverse, many-sided."
    "Provident" is a positive synonym for "miserly." "Officious" is negative: it
    means "acting like an official, sticking your nose into other people's
    business." Finally, both "salubrious" and "affable" are positive, but
    "salubrious" (healthful) is more positive. So (A) is the answer. NOISOME
    means "noxious."

7. CONSECRATE (to make holy) has a positive connotation. The only
    negative word is "curse." The answer is (C). Note: "Destroy" is neutral,
    not negative: you can destroy something that is good or bad.

8. ILLUSTRIOUS has a positive connotation. Now, "bellicose" and
    "ignoble" are equally negative. At this point you have to guess. The
    answer is (B), "ignoble," which means dishonorable. ILLUSTRIOUS
    means "honored, renowned."

9. Since DEIGN starts with DE, it should be negative. So, we are looking for
    a positive word. "Inveigh" is negative; it means to rail against. Eliminate
    (A). "Gainsay" is also negative; it means "to contradict, to impugn."
    Eliminate (B). "Speculate" is neutral as is "reject," rejecting something
    may be wise or unwise depending on the circumstance—eliminate (C) and
    (D). Hence, by process of elimination, the answer is (E). DEIGN means
    "to condescend, to disdain." And LAUD means "to praise, to extol."

10. The prefix "sub" gives SUBTERFUGE the sense of going down. So, we
    expect SUBTERFUGE to have a negative connotation. Hence, we are
    looking for a positive word. Now, "bewilderment" is somewhat
    negative—eliminate. "Artlessness" (sincere, ingenuous) is positive; it may
    be the answer. "Deceit" is negative—eliminate. "Felicitation" (an
    expression of good wishes, congratulation) is also positive; it too may be
    the answer. "Jeopardy" is negative—eliminate. Now, SUBTERFUGE
    means "deceit, conspiracy." The opposite is artlessness. The answer is (B).

Problem Set D:

1. As a verb, CURB means "to restrain or stop." The opposite of stopping an
    activity is encouraging it. Hence, the answer is (B).

2. As a noun, DOCUMENT means "a legal or official paper." But all the
    answer-choices are verbs. As a verb, DOCUMENT means "to attest to, or
    to supply evidence." The opposite is to contradict, which is the meaning of
    "gainsay." The answer is (C).

3. As an adjective, FLUID means "moving in a continuous, smooth manner."
    The opposite would be moving in a hesitating manner, which is the
    meaning of "balky." (Think of a "balk" in the game of baseball.) The
    answer is (D).

4. As a verb, BOLT means "to move quickly." (The sprinters bolted out of the starting blocks.) The opposite is to linger. The answer is (A).

5. As a verb, TABLE means "to postpone." You may have heard it used in government: "Congress tabled the bill." The opposite is to expedite. The answer is (E).

   Choice (D), "propound," is second-best. However, "expedite" is more precisely opposite because it includes the notion of speeding up the consideration of a proposal.

6. As a verb HARBOR mean means "to conceal" (to harbor a criminal). The opposite is to send away, which is the meaning of banish. The answer is (B).

7. As a verb, FLOWER means "to flourish," and the opposite is blight. The answer is (C).

8. As an adjective, STEEP means "precipitous." But as a verb, STEEP means "to saturate." Think of the phrase, "Steeped in tradition." In other words, filled with tradition. The opposite is to dry up, which is the meaning of desiccate. The answer is (A).

9. This is a hard problem. Unfortunately, the common meaning of RENT (payment) will not be tested on the SAT. As a verb, RENT means "to tear apart." The opposite is to RESTORE. The answer is (B).

10. As an adjective, EXACT means "accurate." But as a verb, EXACT means "to use authority to force payment or compliance." The opposite is to CONDONE: to allow or forgive. The answer is (E).

Problem Set E:

1. Legend has it that if you kiss a magical stone in Blarney, Ireland, you will be given the gift of flattering speech, or eloquence. The opposite of BLARNEY, then, is TACITURNITY, which means silence or reticence. The answer is (D).

2. BRAVADO comes from Old Spanish *bravada* or French *bravade*. Someone who shows bravado shows a pretense of bravery. The opposite of a pretense of bravery is true bravery, which is the meaning of VALOR. The answer is (A).

3. BLASÉ is a French word, which means to sicken. The meaning of the word is to become world-weary or apathetic to pleasure or excitement. PROVOKED means to arouse or provide stimulation. The answer is (C).

4. SABOTAGE, a French word, means treason or destruction. To ADVOCATE means to support. The answer is (B).

5. GRATIS comes from Latin, and you may also recognize it from the French word *gratuit*. It means free of charge. EXTRAVAGANT is the opposite of gratis. The answer is (E).

6. PROTÉGÉ comes from the French word *protéger*, which means to protect. A protégé is protected by a mentor, which is the opposite of protégé. One type of mentor is a teacher or PEDAGOGUE. The answer is (B).

7. PEJORATIVE comes from the French word *péjoratif*, which means to worsen. The opposite is ameliorative. The answer is (C).

8. You've heard the saying "Love in any language." The meaning of AMOROUS clearly relates to love. Recall from your undergraduate classes that love in French is *amour*, in Spanish *amor*, and in Italian *amore*. The opposite of love is hate. ABHORRENT means characteristic of loathing. The answer is (A).

9. ACQUIESCE comes from the French word *acquiescer*, which means to consent or agree passively. The opposite of acquiesce is DISSENT. The answer is (E).

10. INCOGNITO is Italian and means unknown or disguised. The word has its roots in the Latin word *cognoscere*, which means to get to know. Add the prefix *in-*, which means "not." You may also remember the Spanish word *conocer* or the French word *connaître*, both of which mean "to know." The opposite of incognito is PALPABLE. The answer is (B).

Sentence Completions

Sentence completions begin each reading section. This is fortunate since the sentence completions are a good warm-up for the harder reading comprehension. The sentence completions form the most straightforward part of the test, and most students do well on them.

Before You Look at The Answer-Choices, Think of a Word That "Fits" The Sentence

Example :

Crestfallen by having done poorly on the SAT, Susan began to question her abilities. Her self-confidence was _____ .

(A)   appeased
(B)   destroyed
(C)   placated
(D)   elevated
(E)   sustained

If somebody is crestfallen (despairing) and has begun to question herself, then her self-confidence would be destroyed. Hence, the answer is (B).

If a Sentence Has Two Blanks, Plug in the First Word in Each Answer-Choice, Eliminating any that Don't Make sense.

After eliminating the answer-choices that don't make sense with the first word plugged in, turn to the remaining answer-choices and plug in the second word.

Example :

The plane had been redesigned so many times before it reached the assembly line that its _____ conception was no longer _____ .

(A)   appropriate . . visible
(B)   dilapidated . . relevant
(C)   original . . recognizable
(D)   initial . . understandable
(E)   promised . . viable

An "appropriate conception" does not make sense in this context, eliminate (A). A "dilapidated conception" probably does not make sense in any context, eliminate (B). A "promised conception" is an odd construction, probably eliminate. Now, "original" and "initial" both work in the first blank. However, "understandable" does not make sense in the second blank. A redesign could clarify the original design, but it's hard to imagine how it would make the original design unintelligible, eliminate (D). Finally, "recognizable" *does* make sense. Since the plane was redesigned many times, is it likely to look quite different from its original design. The answer is (C).

Most often, the answer-choices to sentence completion problems are not simple or common words, that is, words we use in daily speech. Nevertheless, don't hesitate to use a common word. Although an everyday word is unlikely to be the answer, it will help guide you to the answer. Further, it will help eliminate wrong answer-choices.

Be Alert to Transitional Words

Transitional words tell you what is coming up. They indicate that the author is now going to draw a contrast with something stated previously, or support something stated previously.

Contrast Indicators

To contrast two things is to point out how they differ. In this type of sentence completion problem, we look for a word that has the opposite meaning (an antonym) of some key word or phrase in the sentence. Following are some of the most common contrast indicators:

BUT	**YET**
DESPITE	**ALTHOUGH**
HOWEVER	**NEVERTHELESS**
WHEREAS	**IN CONTRAST**

Example :

Although the warring parties had settled a number of disputes, past experience made them _____ to express optimism that the talks would be a success.

(A) rash   (B) ambivalent   (C) scornful   (D) overjoyed   (E) reticent

"Although" sets up a contrast between what has occurred—success on some issues—and what can be expected to occur—success for the whole talks. Hence, the parties are reluctant to express optimism. The common word "reluctant" is not offered as an answer-choice, but a synonym—reticent—is. The answer is (E).

Example :

Rather than increasing its security by developing nuclear weapons, a nascent nuclear power is viewed as a _____ by its enemies.

(A) benefactor   (B) protector   (C) target   (D) patron
(E) nonentity

The phrase "rather than" sets up a contrast between what a country hopes to achieve by developing nuclear weapons (increased security) and what it actually achieves (becoming a target). The answer is (C).

Support Indicators

Supporting words support or further explain what has already been said. These words often introduce synonyms for words elsewhere in the sentence. Following are some common supporting words:

AND	**ALSO**	**INDEED**
FURTHERMORE	**LIKEWISE**	**SIMILARLY**
IN ADDITION	**FOR**	**TRULY**

Example :

Davis is an opprobrious and _____ speaker, equally caustic toward friend or foe—a true curmudgeon.

(A) lofty (B) vituperative (C) unstinting (D) retiring (E) laudatory

"And" in the sentence indicates that the missing adjective is similar in meaning to "opprobrious," which is very negative. Now, *vituperative*—the only negative word—means "abusive." Hence, the answer is (B).

Example :

The belief that sanctions and tactical military strikes can turn the people of a country against a dictator is folly; indeed, as we are witnessing in the Balkans, this _____ causes the population to rally around the dictator.

(A) sometimes (B) rarely (C) invariably (D) never (E) occasionally

"Indeed" in the sentence indicates that the second clause supports and emphasizes what is stated in the first clause: that sanctions and tactical military strikes will not work. Now, something that will not work will *invariably* (always) fail. The answer is (C).

Cause And Effect Indicators

These words indicate that one thing causes another to occur. Some of the most common cause and effect indicators are

BECAUSE	**FOR**	**ACCORDINGLY**
THUS	**HENCE**	**CONSEQUENTLY**
THEREFORE	**IF __ , THEN __ .**	**DUE TO**

Example :

Because the Senate has the votes to override a presidential veto, the President has no choice but to _____ .

(A) object (B) abdicate (C) abstain (D) capitulate (E) compromise

Since the Senate has the votes to pass the bill or motion, the President would be wise to compromise and make the best of the situation. The answer is (E).

Apposition

This rather advanced grammatical structure is very common on the SAT. (Don't confuse "apposition" with "opposition": they have opposite meanings.)

Words or phrases in apposition are placed next to each other, and the second word or phrase defines, clarifies, or gives evidence to the first word or phrase. The second word or phrase will be set off from the first by a comma, semicolon, hyphen, or parentheses. Note: If a comma is not followed by a linking word—such as *and, for, yet*—then the following phrase is probably appositional.

Identifying an appositional structure, can greatly simplify a sentence completion problem since the appositional word, phrase, or clause will define the missing word.

Example :

His novels are _____; he uses a long circumlocution when a direct coupling of a simple subject and verb would be best.

(A) prolix
(B) pedestrian
(C) succinct
(D) vapid
(E) risqué

The sentence has no linking words (such as *because, although*, etc.). Hence, the phrase following the semicolon is in apposition to the missing word—it defines or further clarifies the missing word. Now, writing filled with circumlocutions is aptly described as prolix. The answer is (A).

Example :

Robert Williams' style of writing has an air of _____: just when you think the story line is predictable, he suddenly takes a different direction. Although this is often the mark of a beginner, Williams pulls it off masterfully.

(A) ineptness
(B) indignation
(C) reserve
(D) jollity
(E) capriciousness

There is no connecting word following the colon. Hence, the description, *"just when you think the story line is predictable, he suddenly takes a different direction,"* defines the missing word. Now, something that is unpredictable because it's continually changing direction is capricious. Thus, the answer is (E).

Problem Set:

1. Because of his success as a comedian, directors were loath to consider him for _____ roles.
    (A) supporting
    (B) leading
    (C) dramatic
    (D) comedic
    (E) musical

2. The aspiring candidate's performance in the debate all but _____ any hope he may have had of winning the election.
    (A) nullifies
    (B) encourages
    (C) guarantees
    (D) accentuates
    (E) contains

3. She is the most _____ person I have ever met, seemingly with an endless reserve of energy.
    (A) jejune
    (B) vivacious
    (C) solicitous
    (D) impudent
    (E) indolent

4. Despite all its _____, a stint in the diplomatic core is invariably an uplifting experience.
    (A) merits
    (B) compensation
    (C) effectiveness
    (D) rigors
    (E) mediocrity

5. Liharev talks about being both a nihilist and an atheist during his life, yet he never does _____ faith in God.
    (A) affirm
    (B) lose
    (C) scorn
    (D) aver
    (E) supplicate

6. Existentialism can be used to rationalize evil: if one does not like the rules of society and has no conscience, he may use existentialism as a means of _____ a set of beliefs that are advantageous to him but injurious to others.

   (A) thwarting
   (B) proving
   (C) promoting
   (D) justifying
   (E) impugning

7. These categories amply point out the fundamental desire that people have to express themselves and the cleverness they display in that expression; who would have believed that the drab, mundane DMV would become the _____ such creativity?

   (A) catalyst for
   (B) inhibitor of
   (C) disabler of
   (D) referee of
   (E) censor of

8. This argues well that Erikson exercised less free will than Warner; for even though Erikson was aware that he was misdirected, he was still unable to _____ free will.

   (A) defer
   (B) facilitate
   (C) proscribe
   (D) prevent
   (E) exert

9. Man has no choice but to seek truth, he is made uncomfortable and frustrated without truth—thus, the quest for truth is part of what makes us _____ .

   (A) noble
   (B) different
   (C) human
   (D) intelligent
   (E) aggressive

10. Though most explicitly sexist words have been replaced by gender-neutral terms, sexism thrives in the _____ of many words.

   (A) indistinctness
   (B) similitude
   (C) loquacity
   (D) implications
   (E) obscurity

11. Though a small man, J. Edgar Hoover appeared to be much larger behind his desk; for, having skillfully designed his office, he was _____ by the perspective.
    (A) augmented
    (B) comforted
    (C) apprehended
    (D) lessened
    (E) disconcerted

12. Man is violent and therefore any theory of conflict resolution between nations that _____ to account for this is _____ flawed.
    (A) declines . . supposedly
    (B) refuses . . pejoratively
    (C) fails . . . inherently
    (D) consents . . manifestly
    (E) flinches . . innately

13. Ironically, the foreign affairs policies of democracies are more likely to met with protests than similar policies of totalitarian regimes because a democracy is _____ protest; whereas in a totalitarian regime, no one is listening.
    (A) impassive to
    (B) indifferent to
    (C) imperiled by
    (D) sensitive to
    (E) inured to

14. Although the buildings and streets of this small beach town appear _____, the property values are quite _____ .
    (A) expensive . . steep
    (B) dilapidated . . high
    (C) artistic . . pedestrian
    (D) refurbished . . low
    (E) quaint . . reasonable

15. Though he claimed the business was _____, his irritability _____ that claim.
    (A) sound . . belied
    (B) expanding . . supported
    (C) downsizing . . vindicated
    (D) static . . contradicted
    (E) booming . . affirmed

16. The rules of engagement for United Nations troops stationed in Bosnia prohibit deadly force unless all _____ actions have be exhausted.
    (A) comparable
    (B) menacing
    (C) alternative
    (D) augmented
    (E) extraordinary

17. Despite its lofty goal—truth—many scholars maintain that law as _____ is a highly regulated street fight.
    (A) a dogma
    (B) a study
    (C) a profession
    (D) a philosophy
    (E) a lifestyle

18. The vigorous dispute over where to place a comma in the Republican platform was motivated not by any _____ change in meaning but by a desire not to show any deference to the other side.
    (A) specific
    (B) discredited
    (C) tarnished
    (D) petulant
    (E) infinite

19. The citizenry had become so _____ by the president's _____ that the latest financial scandal did not even make the front page of the newspapers.
    (A) fascinated . . impropriety
    (B) disgusted . . peccadilloes
    (C) distraught . . magnanimity
    (D) regretful . . personification
    (E) jaded . . indiscretions

20. In these politically correct times, it has become _____ to discuss certain subjects at all.
    (A) safe
    (B) eccentric
    (C) precarious
    (D) efficacious
    (E) effortless

21. Although the stock market has experienced strong _____ in the past two years, there have been short periods in which the market has _____ precipitously.

    (A) expansion . . stagnated
    (B) growth . . fallen
    (C) augmentation. . steadied
    (D) extension . . stabilized
    (E) development . . increased

22. Her stern attitude toward the child was complemented with plenty of _____ .

    (A) love
    (B) spite
    (C) indifference
    (D) malice
    (E) ambivalence

23. The interviewer was startled to hear the otherwise gracious author make the _____ remark: "My novels are too sophisticated for the American public."

    (A) apt
    (B) enigmatic
    (C) lofty
    (D) vacuous
    (E) insightful

24. The judge openly associated with racist organizations; nevertheless, he showed no _____ in his decisions during his career.

    (A) favoritism
    (B) benevolence
    (C) openness
    (D) prejudice
    (E) altruism

25. The condemnatory drivel of critics directed toward Steven Spielberg's latest film attests to the fact that the pretentious critics have lost sight of the purpose of movies: _____.

    (A) to exalt
    (B) to correct
    (C) to mislead
    (D) to convert
    (E) to entertain

26. Though in acting circles he has a reputation of being a consummate professional, at times he can be quite _____ on the stage.
    (A) stern
    (B) efficient
    (C) playful
    (D) adept
    (E) aloof

27. Because a comprehensive _____ has yet to be done on the effects of radiation from computer monitors, we don't even know the amount of time the typical office worker spends at a computer monitor.
    (A) theory
    (B) strategy
    (C) solution
    (D) illness
    (E) study

28. The general accused the senator of naiveté for _____ that air strikes alone could stop the aggressors.
    (A) advocating
    (B) denying
    (C) obfuscating
    (D) mishandling
    (E) disallowing

29. Hundreds of citizens showed up to _____ the planning commission's master plan for regional centers, claiming that adding 800,000 additional people to the metro area by the year 2010 would cause overcrowding and gridlock.
    (A) vote on
    (B) protest
    (C) celebrate
    (D) view
    (E) stop

30. Though _____ toward his own needs, he was always magnanimous toward others.
    (A) miserly
    (B) charitable
    (C) profligate
    (D) improvident
    (E) condemnatory

31. The intelligence community should not be _____ for not foreseeing the fall of the Soviet Union; even Hedrick Smith, author of *The Russians*, stated in 1986 that the Soviet Union is the world's most stable society.
    (A) applauded
    (B) contradicted
    (C) faulted
    (D) preempted
    (E) engendered

32. Although prices _____ during the fuel shortage, the suppliers actually saw _____ in profits.
    (A) increased .. a loss
    (B) stabilized .. a boon
    (C) shot up .. an expansion
    (D) fluctuated .. a deprivation
    (E) decreased .. a windfall

33. In the 1950s, integration was _____ to most Americans; now, however, most Americans accept it as _____ .
    (A) welcome .. normal
    (B) an anathema .. desirable
    (C) voluntary .. mandatory
    (D) common .. sporadic
    (E) an abhorrence. . unusual

34. A more admirable character would have been one who overcame his _____ impulses and became good; rather than one who merely lacked the _____ to be bad.
    (A) forbearing .. patience
    (B) ire .. drama
    (C) baser .. intensity
    (D) depraved .. goodness
    (E) evil .. sophistication

35. Although World War II ended more than half a century ago, Russia and Japan still have not signed a formal peace treaty; and both countries have been _____ to develop more _____ relations.
    (A) reticent .. amiable
    (B) inhibited .. colder
    (C) loath .. hostile
    (D) averse .. controversial
    (E) inimical .. blasé

36. The editor found the articles so _____ that he hesitated to print them.

    (A) positive
    (B) comical
    (C) improbable
    (D) indecisive
    (E) interesting

37. Children not only provide cheap labor, but they are also _____, as they do not complain about menial chores given to them or about harsh treatment meted out.

    (A) impertinent
    (B) facile
    (C) presumptuous
    (D) hesitant
    (E) docile

38. Despite its _____ and safety in treating some of the most incapacitating forms of depression and anxiety, it has not been widely _____ .

    (A) security . . renounced
    (B) potency . . repudiated
    (C) ineffectuality . . overtaken
    (D) productivity . . commenced
    (E) usefulness . . accepted

39. Despite her age, she has a silly and _____ sense of humor.

    (A) mature
    (B) trivial
    (C) adolescent
    (D) asinine
    (E) youthful

40. There are different and _____ versions about what happened in the city, but one thing is certain: it a dastardly act that must be condemned _____.

    (A) dissimilar . . concertedly
    (B) contrary . . in unison
    (C) unique . . without conflict
    (D) conflicting . . unequivocally
    (E) complementary . . unanimously

41. By _____ celebrities from the sports, entertainment, or business arenas, the show narrates the stories of the _____ newsmakers from all walks of life.

    (A) displaying . . pedestrian
    (B) profiling . . influential
    (C) parading . . effective
    (D) narrating . . dominating
    (E) setting forth . . ordinary

42. Behind their strange appearance and _____ for carrion, which has long singled them out for fear and loathing, hyenas present a _____ society in which females dominate.

    (A) longing . . contrastive
    (B) penchant . . realistic
    (C) proclivity . . virtual
    (D) appetite . . matriarchal
    (E) yearning . . monarchal

43. At the cutting edge of research, scientists are developing new sunscreens of both _____ and internal varieties.

    (A) polar
    (B) tropical
    (C) territorial
    (D) atmospheric
    (E) regional

44. Although the AIDS epidemic is in the limelight, there is a silent killer _____ through India, killing more people than AIDS itself. The _____ is that, unlike AIDS, this disease is easily cured.

    (A) storming . . satire
    (B) flaming . . ridicule
    (C) raging . . parody
    (D) rampaging . . irony
    (E) traducing . . sarcasm

45. Knowing Julian was overshadowed by many other actors, she knew she was indulging in a bit of _____ when she wondered whether Julian was the greatest living actor ever.

    (A) irony
    (B) overemphasis
    (C) understatement
    (D) hyperbole
    (E) injustice

Answers and Solutions to Exercise

1.	C	10.	D	19.	E	28.	A	37.	E
2.	A	11.	A	20.	C	29.	B	38.	E
3.	B	12.	C	21.	B	30.	A	39.	E
4.	D	13.	D	22.	A	31.	C	40.	D
5.	B	14.	B	23.	B	32.	A	41.	B
6.	D	15.	A	24.	D	33.	B	42.	D
7.	A	16.	C	25.	E	34.	E	43.	B
8.	E	17.	C	26.	C	35.	A	44.	D
9.	C	18.	A	27.	E	36.	C	45.	D

1.   If the public expects a comedian to always make them laugh, then they might not accept a comedian in a serious role. Hence, the directors would be loath (reluctant) to cast a comedian in a dramatic role. The answer is (C).

2.   The phrase "all but" implies that the debate was a make-or-break event for the candidate. Suppose the candidate did well. Then his spirits would be high, and we would expect the missing word to be positive. However, a positive word in the phrase *"all but _____ any hope"* is awkward. Hence, the candidate must have done poorly in the debate and had his hopes for election nixed. So, we turn to the answer-choices looking for "nixed." It's not there, but a synonym—nullifies—is. The answer is (A).

3.   Since no connecting word—such as *and, for, so,* etc.—follows the comma, the phrase *"seemingly with an endless reserve of energy"* defines the missing word. Now, a person with an endless reserve of energy would be lively, which is the meaning of "vivacious." The answer is (B).

4.   "Despite" sets up a contrast between the key phrase "uplifting experience" and the missing word. The implication is that in spite of the rewards, the job is harsh and trying; in other words, rigorous. The answer is (D).

5.   "Yet" draws a contrast between what one would expect an Atheist to do (renounce faith in God) and what Liharev did (maintained faith in God). In other words, he did not lose faith in God. The answer is (B).

6.   To rationalize evil is to make excuses for wrongdoing. Now, the words following the colon explain how existentialism can be used to excuse or justify evil. The answer is (D).

7.   The phrase "who would have believed" implies that the reality is the opposite of what one would expect. Now, one would not expect the drab DMV to be a catalyst for creativity. The answer is (A).

8.   The sentence implies that even when Erikson knows he is taking the wrong path in life, he still cannot stop. That is, he cannot exert free will. The answer is (E).

9.   If man has no choice but to seek truth, then this is an essential characteristic of man. In other words, it is part of what makes us human. The answer is (C).

10.   The sentence is saying that although a word may not be explicitly sexist it may contain sexist connotations or implications. The answer is (D).

11.   The passage states that when sitting behind his desk J. Edgar Hoover looked larger than he actually was. So, the perspective must have increased the appearance of his size. The only word that means to increase is "augmented." The answer is (A).

12.   Since man is violent, any useful theory of conflict resolution must incorporate this fact. The answer is (C).

13.   The clause "whereas in a totalitarian regime, no one is listening" implies that a democracy does listen to protests. In other words, it is sensitive to protests. The answer is (D).

14.   "Although" sets up a contrast between what the property values are (high) and what one would expect them to be in a dilapidated (run down) community. The answer is (B).

15.   If the business was not sound, his irritability would belie (contradict) his claim that the business was sound. The answer is (A).

16.   The word "exhausted" implies that all other actions (alternatives) have been tried. The answer is (C).

17.   The sentence is pointing out that as a practical matter the legal profession pursues the truth through a rough and tumble path. The answer is (C).

18.   The clause "a desire not to show any deference to the other side" implies that the issue was who would win not who was right. So, the placement of the comma did not affect the specific meaning of the sentence. The answer is (A).

19.   A financial scandal is an indiscretion; and it may not have made the front page because the public was jaded (worn out) by an excess of scandals. The answer is (E).

20. The sentence is suggesting that it is risky to discuss certain subjects regardless of what you say. The answer is (C).

21. "Although" sets up a contrast between what happened in the market over a two year period (growth) and what happened in some shorter periods during that time (no growth). The answer is (B).

22. A complement is something that makes up a whole, bringing it to perfection. Of the answer-choices offered, only "love" could complement "stern" in such a manner. The answer is (A).

23. We are told that the author is gracious, yet she makes the churlish comment: "My novels are to sophisticated for the American public." Such an out of character comment is enigmatic. The answer is (B).

24. "Nevertheless" points out a contrast in how the judge felt (prejudice) and how he acted (without prejudice). The answer is (D).

25. The word "pretentious" indicates that the writer believes that the critics take themselves and movies too seriously. That is, the main purpose of a movie is merely to entertain. The answer is (E).

26. "Though" sets up a contrast between the behavior one would expect from a "consummate professional" and the behavior that the actor sometimes displays. Now from a consummate professional, one would expect a serious, work-like attitude, not playfulness. The answer is (C).

27. To determine the amount of time the typical office worker spends at a computer monitor, a study would need to be conducted. The answer is (E).

28. The general is accusing the senator of being naive (unsophisticated) for believing that air strikes alone could stop the aggressors. The answer is (A).

29. People are likely to protest a plan that they believe will cause overcrowding and gridlock. The answer is (B).

30. "Though" sets up a contrast between "magnanimous" (charitable) and "miserly." The answer is (A).

31. The sentence is implying that no one could have foreseen the collapse of the Soviet Union. The answer is (C).

32. The sentence is pointing out that in spite of the higher prices the suppliers lost money. The answer is (A).

33. The sentence is pointing out the difference between the attitudes of people in the '50s and the attitudes today. The answer is (B).

34. The writer is pointing out that one who overcomes evil is more admirable than one who is born simple but good. The answer is (E).

35. If no peace treaty has been signed after 50 years, then the countries are probably reticent (reluctant) to develop more amiable (friendly) relations. The answer is (A).

36. Printing something that is untrue would reflect negatively on the editor, so he hesitated to print the articles because they were "improbable." The answer is (C). "Indecisive" could also be the reason the editor hesitated to print the articles, but "improbable" is a stronger reason not to publish an article. One of the jobs of an editor is to verify the truth of an article. Publishing false material could subject the editor to ridicule or even legal action.

37. The word "as" in the sentence indicates that the missing word is explained or defined by the clause that follows it: "they do not complain about menial chores given to them or about harsh treatment meted out." This aptly describes a "docile" person. The answer is (E).

38. The conjunction "and" in the phrase "Despite its _____ and safety" indicates that the missing word has a positive meaning because "safety" has a positive meaning. Since the sentence is implying that the drug is useful in curing depression and anxiety, it is expected that the drug would be widely used. But "despite" implies that the drug is not widely "accepted." The answer is (E).

39. The word "age" in the sentence implies that the missing word is characteristic of age. "Youthful" fits well: Despite her advanced age, she has a youthful sense of humor. The answer is (E). "Adolescent" could also work in the sentence, but the phrase "adolescent sense of humor" carries a negative connotation, and the sentence does not seem to be critical.

40. The word "and" in the phrase "different and _____ versions" indicates that the missing word is similar in meaning to the word "different." Now, different versions of an event can be "conflicting." Further, a dastardly act needs to be condemned "unequivocally." The answer is (D).

41. The show was organized to tell the stories of successful celebrities. By "profiling" these celebrities, the show narrates the stories of the "influential" newsmakers from all walks of life. The answer is (B).

42. Since hyenas eat carrion (decaying flesh), they have an "appetite" for it. A society ruled by females is called "matriarchal." The answer is (D).

43. The word "both" in the statement implies there are two different types of sunscreen. Since one is internal, the other one should be external or at least of a different type. The choices "territorial," "atmospheric," and "regional" do not imply the opposite of internal. "Polar" and "tropical" may indicate other varieties. Sunscreens are not used in polar regions; they are used in tropical regions. Hence, the answer is (B).

44. The first sentence describes AIDS as a big threat; it also describes another disease that is unreported and is on a greater rampage. Yet, the author says there is a cure for this silent killer. It is ironic that the silent killer causes more harm than AIDS, yet it is curable. The answer is (D).

45. The statement implies that Julian is certainly not the greatest American actor. To believe him to be the greatest actor would be to indulge in "hyperbole." The answer is (D).

www.ingramcontent.com/pod-product-compliance
Lightning Source LLC
Chambersburg PA
CBHW060902280326
41934CB00007B/1159